Overlooked America

DATE DUE

Edited ⸺ ⸺ ᴉe

Copyright 2008 by the American Planning Association
122 S. Michigan Ave., Suite 1600, Chicago, IL 60603

ISBN (paperback): 978-1-932364-50-7
ISBN (hardbound): 978-1-932364-51-4

Library of Congress Catalog Card Number: 2008920526

Printed in the United States of America

Contents

Preface

All of America was riveted—and horrified—when Hurricanes Katrina and Rita struck the Gulf Coast of the U.S. in the late summer of 2005. News reports made it obvious that hundreds of thousands of people lost their homes and businesses, and many lost their lives, because they couldn't outrun the flooding that accompanied the storms. The number of victims was largest in New Orleans, where the poorer neighborhoods were especially flood prone and car ownership was spotty. Without an evacuation plan for those areas, the city made its lower income residents vulnerable to disaster.

Things only got worse in the immediate aftermath of the storms. Emergency providers—including the federal government—were slow to respond, and the poor of New Orleans (and elsewhere) continued to suffer the consequences. Both before and after the hurricanes, their needs simply weren't anticipated. They were overlooked.

They weren't alone in that regard. Although the nation is relatively rich in social services, many individuals and families have needs that aren't being well met. Who are they, and what can planners do to address those needs? The editors of *Planning* magazine set out to find some answers.

What followed was a series of articles published in *Planning* between 2006 and 2008. The title of the series was "Overlooked America." This book includes all of the articles in that series as well as related articles that were published earlier but address the same theme. The articles have been organized into five chapters: The Homeless, Special Needs, The Jobless, Poor Communities, and Katrina Victims. Each chapter includes a brief summary and update. Completely new material appears in the Foreword and Introduction to this book.

Our thanks go to Paul Farmer, FAICP, for writing the Foreword and to Robert Beauregard for contributing the Introduction.

Other contributors include the writers, photographers, and artists who supplied stories and images for the magazine articles and resulting book. Staff members of the Publications Department at the American Planning Association also pitched in—by writing and editing articles and by designing pages. Those involved are editors Meghan Stromberg, Julie Von Bergen, and Ruth Knack, AICP; graphic designers Richard Sessions and Michael Sonnenfeld; and editorial assistant Lowanda Tucker.

Last we must thank W. Paul Farmer, FAICP, the executive director and CEO of the American Planning Association, who had the original idea for the "Overlooked America" magazine articles and book.

Sylvia Lewis
Editor and Publisher, *Planning* magazine
Director of Publications
American Planning Association
January 2008

Introduction

The roots of the U.S. planning profession are deeply embedded in the reform movements of the late 19th and early 20th centuries. During the Progressive Era, the precursors of today's planners addressed the undesirable health, environmental, and commercial consequences of rapid industrialization and urbanization. Lacking the kinds of regulations now in place, urban growth increased the risk of deadly fires, compromised water quality, intensified the slums, threatened property values, and clogged the streets with vehicles—which, in turn, slowed commerce and posed safety risks. For planners, the task was to discipline this chaotic city. To do so they focused on land uses, street layouts, and parks as well as physical plans, building codes, and zoning regulations.

The problems addressed by planners were public problems; yet, the consequences fell disproportionately on some groups and not others. Immigrants were more likely than natives to be crowded into substandard housing and unhealthy neighborhoods, while the poor (unlike the middle class) could not easily flee the city for the countryside when epidemics struck. The target of the incipient planning profession was the physical environments these groups occupied and not the groups themselves. *Physical* reform was on the planning agenda, not *social* reform, although the two were—and are—intimately linked. Planners might have been concerned that particular social groups suffered, but they were less attentive to social distinctions such as immigrant status or whether the factories that despoiled the environment employed adults or children. Rather, physical categories—industrial areas, slums, rail yards, and unpaved streets—were the distinctions used to make sense of the city. The social problems of marginalized and exploited groups were invisible except to settlement houses and social workers.

The planning profession has changed since those Progressive reform years. Today, planners have expanded their gaze beyond the functional challenges of development and the negative externalities of economic activity to include the planning needs of different social groups within the community. Decades ago, and in its most developed state, the focus on the unemployed, the poor, and other disadvantaged groups was known as "social planning." Social planning was a consequence of the political turmoil of the 1960s, the re-discovery of racial discrimination and poverty in the midst of affluence, and the funding patterns of the federal government's War on Poverty. The realization that planners might be complicit in social problems led to a critique of the then-prevailing "bricks-and-mortar" approach to planning, which slashed highways through neighborhoods, demolished inner-city communities, and targeted housing for the middle class, leaving the poor to compete for homes in overcrowded slums or negotiate the meager supply of public housing units.

Advocacy planners called for greater recognition of poor African Americans and troubled youth, among others—groups that had been relegated to the margins during a period of general affluence. Segregated in the inner cities, African Americans found their lives further disrupted by government projects, urban renewal, and highway construction. The fact that minorities lacked planning expertise to resist such harmful government actions was one of the elements that attracted social planners. Drawing on the many initiatives in health planning, mental health planning, day care and education, social services, and job training, advocacy planners took on non-traditional clients. These were not the generalized "users" of the city normally discussed in planning offices but the poor, high school dropouts, the unemployed, unwed mothers, the mentally ill, and the elderly. During the 1960s and 1970s, a significant if numerically small segment of the planning community took social groups, not the physical city, to be the object of their concern.

During these years, many planners were of course taking positions in suburban planning departments or joining consulting firms that provided advice to suburban municipalities. There, in contrast to the cities, social distinctions were less relevant. The residents were young families, mostly white, who were just starting their adult lives and looking forward to years of prosperity. Suburban planners concerned themselves with street plans, subdivision controls, locating schools and ball fields, and the traffic congestion generated by shopping centers. Children and women experienced and used the suburbs differently from men, but, in the early postwar years, this was a minor planning issue.

Social planning waned after the 1970s, once again withdrawing into social work and public health. With the beginning of gentrification in the 1970s, plus the resurgence of the central cities around new office construction, tourism, and entertainment in the 1980s, and downtown housing and mega-projects in the 1990s, city planners turned back to the physical environment as the focal point of the profession. Planners now, and once again, serve the disadvantaged indirectly through affordable housing, community development, and environmental regulations. In effect, and across the history of the planning profession, social groups have been less the targets of planning interventions than the motivation for them. Even recent debates on social justice have focused mainly on the form and physical elements of the city. Planners initially give deprived and marginalized groups center stage, but to them the appropriate policies involve well-located, affordable housing and more supportive neighborhoods—traditional planning responses.

Forces of change

Over the last four to five decades, social distinctions have become more prevalent within planning. This shift was not due solely to shifts within the profession. The forces of change came mainly from the outside. The conservatism of the 1950s and the affluence of the early postwar decades had created a widely shared belief that the entire nation was becoming middle class. When planners rediscovered their reformist roots in the 1960s, however, the U.S. was in the grip of another surge of civic morality. Numerous groups whose access to the country's wealth and opportunities was problematic challenged the social complacency of the era. Most important here was the civil rights movement, with its claim that African Americans were still held down by white society, even if the form of that oppression had changed. Institutional discrimination was unyielding and African Americans lived in the worst neighborhoods, held the lowest paying jobs, and attended the poorest schools. The Declaration of Independence might avow that "all men are created equal," but they certainly were not treated equally. Two societies existed, one black and one white, in a phrase made famous by the Kerner Commission report on the urban riots of the 1960s.

Similar claims of unequal treatment were voiced by Native Americans, gays and lesbians, the disabled, and women. The efforts of the women's movement to add an Equal Rights Amendment to the Constitution were indicative of the times and of a general recognition that people were considered American to a greater and, most importantly, to a lesser degree. In 1962 the socialist critic and activist Michael Harrington pointed to "the other America" of rural poor, ghetto dwellers, and chronically unemployed. Within the American landscape of affluence, Harrington noted, were localities and regions where the economy had essentially collapsed and could no longer generate and distribute the benefits necessary to stave off poverty and psychological deprivation. This was an important observation. The poor were not just disadvantaged in relation to other groups; they lived in different places—places where opportunities were meager.

Recognition of these social differences challenged the core belief that American society was a land of opportunity where one's family background or political connections were trumped by hard work, education, and innate intelligence. The myth was that, because the barriers to advancement were few and idiosyncratic rather than deeply biased, anyone could rise to high status or occupy a position of wealth. Embracing that myth meant that Americans could craft a national identity that drew on the values espoused when the country was first established. During the 20th century, every American—it was widely believed—was or would eventually become middle class in both lifestyle and living conditions.

Working against that myth were claims that Americans did, in fact, make strict social distinctions—and that those distinctions were tightly tied to economic opportunity, discrimination, and political access. Such distinctions undermine the idea that America is a land of opportunity because they point to inequalities and injustices and characterize them as an inevitable consequence of present political and economic arrangements. Paradoxically, without the myth, social inequalities seem less dramatic— and therefore are less likely to be labeled a "pressing social problem."

The background belief in the consensual and homogenizing nature of American society became even more untenable when immigration increased in the 1970s. A much higher percentage of new arrivals were from non-European countries than was the case a century earlier. This re-fueled American xenophobia, and by the 1990s a virulent nativism had returned. Low-skilled immigrants with weak language skills and little education were singled out for particular concern, with Mexicans being the least welcomed (particularly when characterized as illegal). One would have expected African Americans to benefit by comparison and yet the dominant story line became one of "hard-working" immigrants willing to do what African Americans were not willing to do in order to advance up the ladder of social and economic mobility.

Making distinctions among social groups is, of course, an essential part of the complex process of establishing a national identity—a process that involves engaging with others, marketing goods and services, and distributing government benefits. Such distinctions become unacceptable, though, when they are used to oppress people, as when the label "sex offender" becomes the basis for banishment from certain areas of a community. Distinctions also serve to identify who is and who is not profiting from the opportunities and prosperity of American society. In fact, much of what we mean by "overlooked" or the "other America" has to do with a group's tenuous connection to education, employment opportunities, wealth, and health care. The issue is whether or not the group is positioned to live well or is instead marginalized and denied opportunities for advancement.

The poor offer a classic example. Lacking access to well-paid jobs in the formal labor market and, in turn, deprived of political influence to shape public policies to their needs, the poor are on the margins of both the economy and governmental largess. Low-skill immigrants have similar problems, as do those living in depressed rural economies, for example. Homeless adults can be cast in this framework. Many might be burdened by mental illness or brought down by substance abuse, but such afflictions are associated with a prior life of poverty, poor education, and dysfunctional families. A healthy economy is not the solution to all social problems, but in the U.S.—a nation whose government begrudgingly provides welfare benefits and whose public realm is shrinking under the onslaught of neo-conservatism—access to it is crucial to crafting a decent life.

What it means to be overlooked
At the same time, governmental programs are not a panacea. No array of public interventions can solve the social problems of overlooked Americans. Other sectors of society—the family, social support networks, churches—must also be involved. Still, much of what can temper the destitution and despair of those on the margins of the economy comes from governmental assistance as well as government support of nonprofit organizations that provide goods and services to those in need. To be overlooked, then, is to be de-valued within formal labor markets and underserved or ignored by government. In short, the notion of "overlooked" points to what people need in order to live well and to those Americans whose needs are not being met.

Omitted from this formulation are social groups who are overlooked because their particular and often self-asserted identity is unacknowledged—that is, not considered sufficiently "different" by mainstream society. The issue here is not the distribution of opportunities and sharing of wealth but recognition of the group's uniqueness. I am thinking of gay men whose public protests during the late 1960s and thereafter were less about access to housing and jobs and more about having American society acknowledge the validity of their sexual identity. Recognition and tolerance were the objectives. Of course, not all gay men are middle class and gay men have faced, and continue to face, discrimination as regards housing and employment. The major goal of the gay rights movement, though, was the right to be gay in public.

The "mixed race" movement has a similar agenda—a recognition that being multi-racial is different from being mono-racial. And, as with gay men, the quest is for endorsement of this particular social characteristic. Individuals who comprise this category, the argument goes, should be taken into account in census statistics (as they were in the 2000 Census), special education programs, and non-pathological psychological assessments. Gays, mixed race individuals, and other such groups (for example, victims of Japanese American internment during World War II) are "overlooked" in the sense of lacking recognition, but they are not commonly understood as overlooked in terms of their access to resources and opportunities. Identity is the primary issue, not redistribution.

Paradoxically, for a social group to become the object of reform it first has to be overlooked. That is, it has to be recognized as a category of concern. This is not just a matter of searching the social landscape for groups who have drifted outside the mainstream and whose lives are precarious as a result. "Overlooked Americans" are not merely out there ready to be found, as an explorer would discover a "lost" tribe. Rather, they rise to prominence through the political actions of reformers or the protestations of members of the group itself. In academic parlance, they are socially constructed.

This is the case with drunk drivers, people with attention deficiencies, and overweight Americans. Drunk drivers became relevant to policy when the mothers of individuals killed by drunk drivers organized to direct public and political attention to them. And, being overweight became a social problem when analysts calculated the long-term health costs of obesity, Americans began to value exercise and "active lifestyles," and certain body types (the very thin or very muscled) became iconic in advertising. Post-incarceration sex offenders have a similar history. In the past, a person convicted of sexual assault would be punished and then allowed to resume their (now changed) lives, unlabeled. Having been punished, they returned to society, like other offenders. Now, they leave prison and become "sex offenders" for life, placed into a category of concern, not overlooked but heavily scrutinized.

How does this affect the planning profession? Should planners take these different groups into account? Which ones? How?

A planning agenda

Planners, of course, have their own special way of dividing up the world. They view social groups in terms of how they engage with housing, transportation systems, infrastructure, retail centers, and industrial locations. What is asked of social distinctions is whether they have planning implications. From the perspective of planners, homelessness is a matter of shelters and transitional housing, both of which raise zoning issues and often trigger conditional-use permits. For elderly drivers, the issue is the availability of public and para-transit and the consequences of separating land uses versus providing mixed use developments that substitute pedestrian trips for automobile trips. For day laborers, it is the development and location of facilities where they can wait comfortably for work and not signal, as a broken window might do, that the community is in disarray.

In short, planners turn overlooked Americans into planned Americans. Or, to say it differently, the intent of planning is to mediate between the needs of these groups and the physical city. The problem is how to accommodate those needs through planning interventions. Planners are reluctant about straying too far from their core competences and from the public issues about which they have expertise and can speak with authority.

One could argue that this is as it should be. Over the decades, planners in the U.S. have gained support for addressing certain public issues, have developed expertise and competence in these areas, and thus are able to make a public contribution. And, while the boundaries of planning—what is considered a legitimate planning issue and what is not—are fuzzy and thus contentious, the core of planning as defined by law, bureaucratic forms, and professional norms is fairly well-established. This is fine. Still, the planning profession needs to be flexible, willing to adapt to changing conditions, and open to innovation.

Not to be forgotten is that other professions exist to address the social needs overlooked by planners. The traditional response to this has been to call for planners to better coordinate with government, nonprofits, and other experts, because planners belong to the only profession that cares about and understands the city in its entirety, taking the role of facilitator. Yet, any emphasis on "overlooked Americans" is likely to pose problems.

First of all, identifying an overlooked group means extracting it from the milieu in which it exists and thus from the multi-dimensionality of social life. This occurs when the rural poor are presented independently of the rural affluent; when homeless youth appear and their non-homeless parents are relegated to the background. Any good planner knows that to address the issue of day laborers, one also has to recognize immigrants, local homeowners, do-it-yourself big box stores, and local contractors. Which one is "the problem" that is overlooked? An argument could be made that the prior and more consequential issue is the relationship between local contractors and their homeowner clients, not the day laborers.

A second denial of complexity occurs when a person is characterized, for example, as a displacee from public housing and thus slotted into this category as his or her primary identification. For planning and policy purposes—for purposes of reform—it might well be the most salient characteristic. Yet, any direct contact with displacees would lead quickly to the realization that other personal and social traits are equally relevant. This is not to imply that overlooked Americans have multiple problems. But, if one takes seriously a concern with people and their lives, then one has to engage them in a fuller way than simply as a category of concern. A displacee might also be employed, caring for aging parents across town, or active in the local neighborhood association. These are important factors for providing assistance.

This discussion points to the limits of both social reform and of planning. To design planning tools and public policies to account for the multiplicity of identities and responsibilities that any person has would be to bring the whole process of reform to a full stop. Forced to treat a person as an individual, few would be helped. Public and nonprofit interventions are simply not designed to do this. Hence the need for categories, but which ones and how encompassing should they be?

And thus back to planning, which, like reform, must rely on categories to do what needs to be done. In planning, the parallel "ideal" would be to treat each piece of property in its fullest social and economic extension. This, though, would turn planning away from grasping the core dynamics of the cities and suburbs while burdening it with so much detail that piecemeal planning would reign. This is not what planning is meant to do and not what cities need from planners. Consequently, planners are inclined to use broad categories and avoids particularities, for only in that way can a proper overview of physical development be realized. And yet, planners do move between large visions and narrow issues—for example, from a small number of land-use categories to the designation of historic districts and the consequences of an ill-placed curb cut. The solution is to append exceptions to rules.

Even as planners pay more and more attention to the social roots of planning problems, they hold to their concern for the physical environment and remain committed to a world in which such categories as land use, transportation, housing, environment, and zoning make conceptual and practical sense. Thus, we are left with the importance of the category of the "overlooked Americans" as well as an appreciation of its specific role within planning practice. Planners can hardly plan without an understanding of the way in which different groups draw support from, and live well within cities, suburbs, and small towns. And although planning's historic inclination has been to plan for the norm, its reformist inclination is to addresss the consequences of injustice that privilege some Americans while marginalizing others.

Robert A. Beauregard
Professor of Urban Planning and Director of the Urban
Planning Program
Graduate School of Architecture, Planning, and Preservation
Columbia University
New York City

December 2007

Foreword

As the tragedy of Hurricane Katrina emerged over several days, searing images touched both citizens of America and citizens of the world. A set of images—people on rooftops, people on highway overpasses, people at the Superdome—reminded us of despair and neglect. Another image— President George W. Bush pensively looking at the catastrophe from an airplane window after he had finally interrupted his Crawford Ranch vacation—came to represent the gulf between need and response. President Bush's approval ratings would never recover. But would those on the rooftops and overpasses ever recover? What about similar victims of other disasters throughout the U.S.? What about those that suffer daily at the hands of an economy, a political system, and a belief system that too often are unresponsive to so many basic human needs? Shouldn't America again aspire to be a nation of human dignity for all?

Shortly after Hurricanes Katrina and Rita had devastated New Orleans and an area the size of the United Kingdom, I was speaking in another U.S. city about the disaster. A couple of questioners from the audience asked questions I had heard before: "Why wasn't New Orleans prepared? How could those people in Louisiana have neglected their own? What would you expect in the South?" That morning, I had picked up a copy of the local newspaper and I was quickly able to point out to the questioners at least five articles that raised quite similar questions about their city. Unfortunately, that probably would have been the case in almost any U.S. city in 2005.

Overlooked America tells stories. The stories may not be about important people as defined by either the radio or pop culture. They are stories about the many in America who struggle to lead decent, dignified, productive lives, often against enormous odds. Good people can sometimes make bad decisions. Collectively, we should strive to make good decisions at the national level, in the states, and back home in our communities. In overlooking those described in the following chapters, we are also over-looking someone else—ourselves. Our own human dignity can only exist in an environment of respect and caring. The stories that follow are stories about all of us.

W. Paul Farmer, FAICP
Executive Director and CEO
American Planning Association
February 2008

CHAPTER

1

The Homeless

Why is anyone homeless in the U.S.? How many homeless Americans are there? Where do they reside? What can be done to help them? Anyone seeking the answers must realize that homelessness has roots in social problems and that planning is one way to address them.

People become homeless for many reasons: lack of income, lack of family support, disabilities, a shortage of affordable housing, and natural disasters among them. Although the homeless may be more numerous and more visible in cities, they also reside in rural areas. In some cases, the homeless may have shelter but it is temporary; they are doubling up with family or friends and could be turned away at any time.

An accurate census of the homeless is virtually impossible. Estimates put the number as high as 3.5 million in any given year, according to federal sources and others.

Among the solutions being attempted nationwide are permanent supportive housing (which includes social services and job counseling as well as shelter) and affordable housing of various sorts, including single room occupancy units with private kitchens and baths. Sometimes enlightened employers provide housing as well—as is true for a few of the growers who hire migrant workers.

Figure 1-1
The six-story, $13.3 million Villa Harvey Mandel opened in San Diego in 2003. Its 90 units are home to some of the city's hardest-to-serve residents. A large stained glass mosaic designed by artist Italo Botti, entitled "Neighbors Helping Neighbors," covers one side of the building complex. Source: Father Joe's Villages

A ROOF OF ONE'S OWN

Homelessness is growing, but solutions are out there.

By Jim Romeo

Tony, 48 years old, spent 15 years as a Navy yeoman and now receives $361 a month in disability payments from the Veterans Administration. He panhandles for extra cash around Norfolk, Virginia, and has been homeless for three years.

Tony is far from alone. According to a survey announced in early October by *USA Today*, more than 727,000 individuals were homeless in 460 communities last spring.

However, about 3.5 million Americans are likely to experience homelessness in any given year—not counting the many thousands set adrift after Hurricanes Katrina and Rita decimated the Gulf Coast this summer. Billions in emergency funds are being spent to help the hurricane victims, and billions more are spent each year to control the nation's perennial homelessness problem.

The Bush administration's proposed budget for fiscal 2006 includes $28.5 billion for homelessness programs administered through HUD and a $1 billion increase for Section 8 housing. It also includes $1.4 billion for Homeless Assistance Grants, $200 million more than in 2005. Altogether, the administration has requested $4 billion in 2006 for federal housing and social programs for the homeless—an increase of 8.5 percent.

Homelessness was growing even before Hurricane Katrina made it worse. In 1997, research conducted in 11 communities and four states by the National Coalition for the Homeless found that shelter capacity had more than doubled in nine communities and three states in the previous decade.

Housing first

According to Dan Straughan, executive director of the Homeless Alliance in Oklahoma City (which has an estimated 1,200 to 1,500 homeless residents), ideas about housing the homeless are changing. He says that the old model is based on a continuum of care that begins in an emergency homeless shelter, where the newly homeless get shelter, food, clothing, and access to government and nonprofit services. Those ready to move on typically go to transitional housing and then to permanent housing, often with financial support.

However, many communities, notably large metropolitan areas on the East and West coasts, have taken a different tack in the last five to 10 years. Their approach, called "housing first," moves the homeless person into supportive housing immediately. The aim is to get homeless individuals off the streets and into a self-supportive culture that will keep them housed and self-reliant.

"The thought is that it's a lot more likely that a person will work on their problems if they're in an apartment or single-room occupancy facility rather than in a cavernous barracks with 100 other people with the same and worse problems," explains Straughan. "Some really good longitudinal research indicates that this approach can be both cost-effective and successful."

He cites a study by the Lewin Group, a national health care and human services consulting firm based in Falls Church, Virginia, which examined the daily cost of supportive housing in nine cities: San Francisco, Los Angeles, Atlanta, New York, Chicago, Boston, Seattle, Phoenix, and Columbus, Ohio. The results of the study, issued in November 2004, showed that a day in supportive housing costs significantly less than a day in jail or in a psychiatric hospital, and a day in permanent supportive housing costs even less than a day in a shelter.

The Fannie Mae Foundation and the Corporation for Supportive Housing, a nonprofit based in New Haven, Connecticut, followed 4,679 people placed in supportive housing and found that their total annual unit costs were $17,277—or nearly $6,000 less than it takes to house an individual in a shelter, according to figures compiled by the New York-based Coalition for the Homeless.

"A formerly homeless person in stable housing is twice as likely to be employed," says Straughan, "twice as likely to be physically and mentally healthy, to be free from substance abuse, and to stay out of jail, than a homeless person either in the shelter system or on the street."

Portland, Oregon, is one city that is embracing the housing first approach. In a report issued December 2004, *Home Again: A Ten Year Plan to End Homelessness in Portland and Multnomah County*, the city states that "the most critical issue that faces all homeless people—the lack of permanent housing—will be addressed first. Other services and programs directed at homeless people and families will support and maintain homeless people in this permanent housing."

The report sets an ambitious goal for the city and county: to create 2,200 new permanent supportive housing units for chronically homeless individuals and homeless families with special needs by the year 2015.

To accomplish these goals, the city will focus on three specific areas: First, it will attend to the problems of the most chronically homeless. Then it will streamline access to existing services in an effort to prevent further homelessness—for example, by seeking more partnerships with nonprofits. Finally, it will put resources into specific programs that offer measurable results.

The emerging homeless
In the midst of the current real estate bubble, more and more families are becoming homeless, says Joan Noguera, executive director of the Nassau-Suffolk Coalition for the Homeless on Long Island—the suburban area east of New York City. "We have a housing market that has gone sky high," she says.

She points out that Long Islanders have a median income of $85,000, yet many wage earners don't earn 30 percent of that figure. The region is home to some of the nation's most affluent communities, but some 40,000 individuals are homeless. Two-thirds of those are members of families; half are children. According to data released by the Urban Institute in 2000, children make up about 39 percent of the homeless population nationally.

*Figure 1-2
Students and faculty at Auburn University have found a way to convert steel shipping containers into shelters that can be trucked and assembled quickly—making them useful for temporary housing. Source: D.K. Ruth, Auburn University*

Noguera cites an example of a single mother with children who is currently in a homeless shelter and is seeking a rental unit for $900 per month—hard to find on suburban Long Island. To secure an apartment, she needs the first month's rent plus two months' security deposit—or $2,700. The coalition was trying to help her, but without the funds, she and her children would remain in a shelter.

Families composed 41 percent of the urban homeless population, according to a U.S. Conference of Mayors survey completed in 2004. This was an increase of five percent over the two previous years. "The face of homelessness has changed," said James Garner, mayor of the village of Hempstead, Long Island, when the survey was released. Garner is a past president of the mayors' conference.

New York as a whole seems to be on the right track. Linda Gibbs, commissioner of the city's Department of Homeless Services, recently announced that from December 2004 to May of this year, the number of people in the city's homeless shelters dropped by 2,379 individuals, the largest decline in any six-month period since 1990. The number of homeless children dropped by 13 percent, from 15,766 in May 2004 to 13,770 in May 2005. These results put the city ahead of an aggressive target set by Mayor Michael Bloomberg to reduce homelessness by two-thirds over a five-year period.

Services are crucial

"In my view, large-scale homelessness of the kind we have seen over the past 25 years is primarily attributable to the policy of deinstitutionalizing the mentally ill," says Seth Forman, AICP, deputy director of the Long Island Regional Planning Board. Forman believes that homelessness has less to do with housing markets than with poor mental health, addiction, and physical abuse.

Advocates for the homeless agree that services are crucial. That means services to enhance life skills and budgeting skills and rehabilitation for drugs and alcohol. Affordable housing without such services is not likely to work, the experts say.

Father Joe's Villages, a faith-based nonprofit organization in San Diego, follows that premise. Its founder, Father Joe Carroll, won the American Planning Association's Paul Davidoff Award for advocacy in 1997. The organization's innovative formula for programs and services has been endorsed as a prototype by the Department of Housing and Urban Development.

A recent project developed by Father Joe's Villages is Villa Harvey Mandel, opened in May 2003. It is a $13.3 million, six-story affordable housing development with 90 units that provides a home to the "hardest-to-serve" community members, with residents ranging from the extremely low-income and formerly homeless to those with chronic physical disabilities, substance abuse problems, and mental illness. The project was awarded the "2004 Special Needs Housing Project of the Year" by the San Diego Housing Federation.

Units vary in size from 326-square-foot studios to 540-square-foot one bedrooms, with many of the west-facing apartments offering views of the Coronado Bridge, Petco Park, and downtown San Diego. The development also features the world's largest glass mosaic, titled "Neighbors Helping Neighbors: A Tribute to Donors, Volunteers, and Staff."

Support services are offered at the nearby St. Vincent de Paul Village, also affiliated with Father Joe's Villages. Services include medical and dental care, counseling, job training and placement services, legal assistance, information and referral, and assistance with entitlement programs.

Eight of the units at Villa Harvey Mandel are designated Shelter Plus Care units for formerly homeless single adults with disabilities. Some 25 beds are reserved for single adults who have mental illness or are chemically dependent. At the time of application, all prospective special needs residents must complete a certification form verifying their disability or special needs. Many residents are both substance abusers and have a mental illness.

Getting project approval wasn't easy. To combat negative perceptions, Father Joe's Villages met many times with East Village and Barrio Logan groups. The city council approved the project by a single vote. Construction began in April 2002.

Figure 1-3
Each shelter measures 40 by 8 feet and costs about $2,500. Source: D.K. Ruth, Auburn University

Speed it up

Permit processing for affordable housing is her agency's biggest headache when it comes to dealing with homelessness, says Marcella Escobar, deputy director of San Diego's Development Services, a branch of the city's planning department. "Fast tracking the permit process has been the focus that our department has taken. We realize that time is of the essence," she says.

That's where the affordable housing expediting program comes in. "In the past we had situations where [permitting] would take six months to a year, if not longer," Escobar says. With the expediting program, some projects have received discretionary approvals and gotten to a public hearing within three months, she adds.

The city of San Diego works hand in hand with various social organizations and community and faith-based groups to assist the city's homeless population. It is also renowned for developing single-room-occupancy housing—the type of housing that can prevent homelessness because the units are affordable to people with very modest incomes.

In my backyard?

Community Housing Works, a local nonprofit organization near San Diego, is mindful of the problems caused by the not-in-my-backyard syndrome. Sue Reynolds, the organization's executive director, says her group works with the surrounding community through a board of directors that includes local residents, businesses, and government officials.

One of the group's projects, the Marisol Apartments in Oceanside, California, won APA's Paul Davidoff Award in 1999. Everyone living in the 21 apartments there is HIV-symptomatic or has AIDS. Ten apartments are reserved for the homeless. Rents range from about $110 to $300 a month, and the apartments serve residents with monthly incomes of $330 to $1,000.

The project wasn't greeted with universal approval, Reynolds says, but her group used what she calls "old-fashioned community work" to turn the tide. It managed to convince neighbors that the new project would be better than what it was replacing.

"In many communities, the faith-based community is doing the lion's share of the day-to-day work with the homeless," says Dan Straughan. "The nonprofit community is also deeply involved. It behooves a city planning department to become (or get access to) a community convenor—that is, an organization that can bring many groups together to reach a consensus on how to best attack a problem."

A last word from Straughan: Bureaucracy is the enemy of housing solutions, which face what he calls the three Bs of homeless funding: "It's byzantine in its complexity, burdensome in the amount of oversight required to administer, and blind to local community need."

Jim Romeo is a freelance writer based in Chesapeake, Virginia. This article was published in December 2005.

Instant Shelter

According to various counts, 500,000 individuals were left homeless by Hurricanes Katrina and Rita, which struck the Gulf Coast in August and September. Homelessness caused by a natural disaster requires a swift response and practical solutions.

While thousands of evacuees have fled to other parts of the country, many want to stay closer to home. Technology is helping to make that happen.

World Shelters for Humanitarian Needs, based in Arcata, California, is sending some of its portable Quonset hut-style shelters to the Gulf Coast. PVC pipe, retaining clips, and plastic sheeting are the materials used in these temporary shelters, which can house medical clinics or become makeshift residences, as needs dictate.

Similar shelters have been used in Sri Lanka, Indonesia, in India, and for the tsunami relief efforts. According to the organization, $365 covers the cost of a complete 23-foot by 11-foot shelter with floor and doors. In early September, World Shelters donated over 60 shelters and "autonomous living units" to the Biloxi–Gulfport region. They will be used by the Harrison County Fire Department to house their firefighters and relief workers assisting the displaced.

In Alabama, students and faculty at Auburn University's College of Architecture, Design and Construction have converted shipping containers into makeshift shelters at a cost of about $2,500 each. The containers measure 40 feet by 8 feet by 9 feet and are made with wooden floors. The shelters would require community kitchens and sanitary facilities if FEMA decides to embrace their use.

Georgia-based Habitat for Humanity has launched Operation Home Delivery, a project that allows volunteers to ship housing components such as roofs, walls, and foundations fitted with electrical and plumbing systems to the Gulf Coast for reconstruction. The homes range from 1,100 to 1,300 square feet and have two or three bedrooms. The first "house in a box" was delivered to Slidell, Louisiana, in October.

GIS is also helping in the post-hurricane shelter effort. The Urban and Regional Information Systems Association has deployed more than 800 volunteers known as the URISA Geographic Information Systems Corps to assist in the Gulf Coast cleanup. Most are working at the University of Mississippi's Emergency Operations Center. Like World Shelters, the GIS Corps has been deployed overseas.

How Does One Become Homeless?

According to Dan Straughan, executive director for Oklahoma City's Homeless Alliance, the causes of homelessness are varied:

• Growing substance abuse, especially with the rise of inexpensive, highly addictive drugs like methamphetamine and crack cocaine. Drug use obviously is a financial drain and often causes job loss. The combination often causes homelessness.

• Lack of access to mental health care. Mental illness continues to be undertreated. In Oklahoma City, 48 percent of the homeless are mentally ill, abusing substances, or both.

• Decreasing rates of health insurance. As the cost of providing health insurance escalates, fewer companies, especially small businesses, cover their employees. One in five of the homeless in Oklahoma City cite a medical expense as a leading cause of their homelessness.

• Lack of affordable housing. "Affordable" typically means "affordable to people making 70 percent of the area's median income." If a person with severe mental illness or a physical disability is receiving Supplemental Security Income or Social Security Disability Income, they are more likely getting only 30 percent of the area's median income.

• Other contributing factors: a growing population of ex-offenders reentering society, natural disasters, and economic downturns.

Resources

In print. See the October 12, 2005 issue of *USA Today* for details about the homeless in 460 communities nationwide. Earlier this year, at HUD's request, those places took "street counts," not just a census of people in shelters. HUD has not yet released the results of those counts, but *USA Today* published the total after contacting each locale.

See future issues of *Planning* for details about recovery efforts after Hurricanes Katrina and Rita. San Diego's single-room occupancy housing is highlighted in *Making Places Special*, by Gene Bunnell (published in 2002 by APA's Planners Press). For information on Father Joe's Villages, see the April 1997 issue of *Planning*. The Marisol Apartments were described in the April 1999 issue.

On the web. The Lewin Group's study on the cost of supportive housing is at www.lewin.com. Portland's *Home Again* report is at www.portlandonline.com/shared/cfm/image.cfm?id=66995. See www.nyc.gov for data from New York City's Department of Homeless Services. World Shelters is at www.worldshelters.org.

A RURAL PROBLEM, TOO

Homelessness beyond the big cities

By Paul Rollinson, AICP

Brenda knew Springfield, Missouri, before she eventually moved there to get help at The Kitchen, Inc., the city's largest homeless shelter. She finished junior high and high school in this mid-sized city (pop. 150,000), which is set within a largely rural region. Before she arrived at the shelter, her life had been a series of ups and downs—mostly downs, to hear her tell the story.

Before returning home to live with her aging parents in a rural community not far from Springfield, Brenda married, had two children, got divorced, and then experienced a number of abusive relationships. For a time she had lived in West Virginia: "I made a bad choice to go out there with my boyfriend, and it was a really bad, bad situation," she says. When asked if she was abused, the answer was: "Emotionally, yes. And sexually, yes, and verbally, yes." Brenda's details are gut-wrenching to listen to. Upon leaving, she says, "The only place I had to live was with my Mom and Dad."

Once she was living with her parents, she discovered that her husband did not, in fact, have custody of her two children, now ages 14 and 18: "I saved all my money to get a bus ticket [out of town] to get the girls. I brought them back," she says. "They wanted to be with me. They didn't want to be with their Dad; he was a crackhead—still is, for all I know. He was giving my oldest daughter drugs; she ended up in the hospital one time."

So Brenda's two daughters joined her, and all three of them were then living with her parents. "We didn't have enough dressers, enough places to hang clothes. I had to sleep on the couch," Brenda says. "It was not a good place; there was tension because my Mom was trying to tell me how to run my life and my kids' life. And my Mom and Dad were bickering all the time."

Brenda (not her real name) and her girls were forced to stay with her parents because they had nowhere else to go, but the situation got intolerable: "After my Dad exploded one night, I just couldn't live at home anymore," she says.

Pushed to the edge, Brenda decided to consider her options in Springfield. Realizing she had few choices, she considered the homeless shelter: "I knew that this was a shelter, but I never really thought about it being a home for me. I decided to call and make an appointment and come and look it over."

Brenda never thought that this was where she'd end up, but, she says, "After I saw it, took a tour, saw the room, I said fine, this is really good. And I am here." Her parents did not want her to move to the shelter, she says, "but I told them that this is the only door that has been opened and I am going to choose to take that. I'm learning to be more assertive."

Rural homeless remain hidden

The homeless in rural areas and smaller towns and cities have largely been overlooked. Their problems have often taken a back seat to the more glaring problems evident in big cities.

People who are homeless in rural America rarely fit the national stereotype. While some are literally homeless, the majority are living in extremely precarious housing situations. They are often moving from one overcrowded, or barely affordable, housing situation to another, often doubling up or tripling up with family or friends.

Some sleep in vehicles or in other improvised housing. Some camp in isolated areas and some are families who are facing foreclosure and imminent eviction from their homes.

The rural homeless are often less visible than their urban counterparts, partly because of lower population densities in rural areas and the scarcity of social services and shelter programs to identify and assist them. Although the rural homeless are not as concentrated or as visible as the urban homeless, proportionally there may be more of them in many rural areas.

As a whole, the nation's rural population has lower income, lower employment, and higher poverty levels than urban and suburban Americans. Many rural Americans have experienced economic downturns not seen since the Great Depression, with dwindling populations and growing fiscal problems. Remote and farm-dependent counties appear to be facing especially difficult challenges.

Poverty rates have been consistently higher in nonmetropolitan areas. Of the 386 persistently poor counties—those with 20 percent or more of their populations living in poverty as measured in the 1970 through 2000 censuses—340 are nonmetropolitan. The majority are in parts of the U.S. where poverty primarily reflects conditions among racial or ethnic minority groups or the predominantly white population of the Southern Highlands, mostly the Allegheny and Cumberland Plateau counties of Kentucky and West Virginia, plus parts of the Ozark Plateau and Ouachita Mountains west of the Mississippi.

Unfortunately, the social problems of rural Americans have received less attention than their more visible urban counterparts. Many Ameri-

Figure 1-4
Jose Adrian Tenahua lives with other homeless men and women in a tent city in
Ocean County, New Jersey. His encampment is one of several erected in the woods
near towns along the Jersey Shore. Source: Tyler Hicks, The New York Times

cans view life in rural communities as bucolic, but this image is partially
maintained by the invisibility of our rural citizens in need.

Estimates from different sources show that in the late 1990s at least 2.3
million, and perhaps as many as 3.5 million, people experienced homelessness at some time during an average year. Rural homelessness is estimated
to make up anywhere from seven to 14 percent of this population. *Helping
America's Homeless*, a widely referenced Urban Institute study by Martha
Burt and others, puts the number at nine percent. The rural homeless are
less likely to live on the street or in a shelter, and are more likely to live in
car, or with relatives or friends in overcrowded or substandard housing.

The problems inherent in these estimates begin with the definition of
the homeless and the techniques used in counting them. The most popular
counting technique is a census of the individuals staying in shelters and
recognized congregation sites. While this method may be acceptable for
getting estimates of the homeless population in large metropolitan areas,
it does not do justice to rural homeless populations.

One of the main problems in rural areas is that the homeless become invisible, or unrecognizable in rural settings. Homeless shelters and service providers are few and far between, often leaving only family and limited community assistance available to those in need.

To date, a significant number of national, state, and local organizations have endorsed the call for the U.S. Department of Housing and Urban Development to adopt a definition of homelessness that is broader and would more accurately reflect the experience of homeless persons in rural areas. Currently, the HUD definition excludes people who are forced to stay with others temporarily (those who are "doubled-up"). These include Brenda and her daughters and people staying in motels because they have no other options.

In search of help

The rural homeless like Brenda are often forced to move in search of help. In smaller communities across the U.S., the homeless have become more visible in places that are ill-prepared to assist them. Debates are under way in many of these communities concerning the provision of homeless services and the so-called "attraction" of this population. Today, the connection between residency and public assistance has reemerged as states and localities worry about providing services that may be a magnet for the homeless.

More than half of the homeless in Springfield who were surveyed in 1999 came from the southwest region of Missouri, and two-thirds originated from within the state. Overall, three-quarters came from the four states of Arkansas, Kansas, Missouri, and Oklahoma.

Springfield is the retailing and service center of the Ozarks. The area served by the large multiservice homeless shelter extends throughout a large portion of this mostly rural state. If such a phenomenon as a homeless social-service magnet exists, this organization would be one.

However, the vast majority of homeless individuals were not traveling to the shelter from other states. They originated in the predominantly rural communities of the wider region, where social services—especially for those fleeing domestic violence or other crises—were very limited. A small regional network of agencies does exist, but they all reported insufficient funds to support all service provision requests.

The rural and small town homeless are different from the homeless in larger cities. For one thing, there are many more homeless families in nonmetropolitan areas than in many metropolitan settings. They are also more likely to be white families and single mothers with children, working and homeless for the first time.

Rural homelessness is the result of poverty and the lack of affordable housing. Research published by the Rural Poverty Research Center in

Figure 1-5
The Kitchen, Inc., is a
multiservice agency in
Springfield that started in
1983, eventually buying
several buildings. Source:
The Kitchen, Inc.

2004 notes that the odds of being poor are between 1.2 and 2.3 times higher for those in non-metroplitan areas.

Many wind up homeless because of the problems associated with doubling up in overcrowded housing. In Springfield, the number of those who had previously been living in shelters or on the streets was very low. The homeless who were studied in Springfield in 1999 were more likely to be precariously housed with friends or relatives than visible on the streets, and this is one of the reasons rural homelessness has been largely overlooked by researchers and policy makers alike.

Violence prevalent

The problem involves more than the lack of a roof. Decent, safe, and affordable housing is obviously a necessity for those who find themselves homeless in rural areas, but their needs go beyond housing. The self-reported reasons for homelessness underestimated the extent of disabilities and family violence—factors that became more obvious when the Springfield shelter's intake data were analyzed.

Self-reported reasons given for homelessness:

Disability	11%
Eviction	21%
Family breakup	17%
Family violence and abuse	2%
Financial problems	31%
Other	18%

Even though 11 percent of the population claimed they were homeless because of a disability, the number found in the in-depth analysis of the narratives describing their pathways to the shelter was much higher. Nearly two-thirds had a history of substance abuse, one-half had a history of mental illness, and almost one-fourth had a medical problem. These data suggest that disability is very common among the rural homeless. (Other studies have shown that disability is also common among the urban homeless.)

The variable that was most commonly associated with the rural homeless was family violence, despite the fact that only two percent reported it as the reason for their homelessness. In Springfield, more than 68 percent of the women interviewed had experienced family violence. Physical abuse was the most common form of family violence, although 20 percent experienced emotional abuse and 13 percent experienced sexual abuse.

Brenda's self-reported reason for homelessness is typical. While she reported her reason for homelessness as family breakup, it was not until we interviewed her several times that we learned the true nature of her breakup.

Histories of abuse and violence are very difficult to cope with, and a typical response is repression and denial. The abuses identified in the narratives of the intake interviews make it quite clear that domestic violence is a significant variable in explaining the pathways many rural families take to homelessness.

Brenda initially saw domestic violence as typical and even acceptable. "It is only now that I see the pattern and the trends," she says. Caught in a storm, many suffering from domestic violence do not know how to reach out or even where to go.

Paul Rollinson teaches urban geography and social planning at Missouri State University. He is the coauthor of *Homelessness in Rural America*, published in 2006. This article was published in June 2007.

Things to Be Done

The rural homeless face many special challenges:

- A dispersed and often hidden population
- Limited transportation, making outreach and coordination difficult
- Federal programs that favor the homeless in larger metropolitan areas
- Lack of affordable housing and rental assistance
- Nonexistent or shrinking mental health and drug and alcohol services
- Limited capacity for resource development, including grant writing and management

To meet some of these challenges rural areas need:

- Formal coordination of outreach centers and engagement teams
- Access to information on best practices
- Grant-writing and management assistance

Resources

In print. *Homelessness in Rural America: Policy and Practice.* Paul A. Rollinson and John T. Pardeck. 2006. Haworth Press. The book describes shelter intake data in 1,480 cases of homeless households using the services of The Kitchen, Inc., in Springfield, Missouri, in 1999. One-fifth of the narratives (296 cases) were reviewed to learn about pathways to homelessness, and another 10 percent of the homeless (30 cases) were interviewed multiple times and cross referenced with key informants to create a triangulated qualitative analysis of the nature of rural homelessness.

Helping America's Homeless: Emergency Shelter or Affordable Housing? Martha Burt, Laudan Aron, Edgar Lee, and Jesse Valente. 2001. Urban Institute Press. This book describes homeless people and service systems across the nation using data from the National Survey of Homeless Assistance Providers and Clients, conducted by the Urban Institute in 1996. It is unique in its breadth and coverage and offers a comprehensive look at homeless assistance programs. It covers urban, suburban, and rural homelessness.

Out of Sight, Out of Mind: Homeless Children and Families in Small Town America. Yvonne M. Vissing. 1996. University Press of America. This book details the causes and consequences of homelessness among school-aged children and their families in five New Hampshire communities. Published after six years of sociological investigation during the 1990s, this book is rich in insights and descriptions of the complexity of the problem.

On the web. Housing Assistance Council: www.ruralhome.org; National Coalition for the Homeless: www.nationalhomeless.org; National Alliance to End Homelessness: www.endhomelessness.org; National Center for Homeless Education: www.serve.org/nche; Rural Poverty Research Center: www.rprconline.org; Pennsylvania's Rural Homeless Reality: www.ruralpa.org/Homeless.pdf.

MIGRANT, NOT HOMELESS

By James B. Goodno

Jesus Ortiz spent his first season as a migrant farmworker in California sharing a roughly 10- by-10 foot room with his father and nine other men. This year, the 19-year-old shared a comparable room with just his father. The difference: The two men arrived early enough in the harvest season to grab a pair of beds in a small housing project. That project was developed for migrants by the Coachella Valley Housing Coalition and the Riverside County Economic Development Authority.

The Ortizes were lucky. Las Mañanitas can house 128 men in 16 units. The vast majority of the 15,000 migrants who arrive in this southern California desert valley for the annual table-grape harvest must fend for themselves. Some crowd into rented garages, apartments, trailers, and motel rooms. Others camp in parks, parking lots, and by irrigation canals, living in what a federal Housing and Urban Development official calls Third World conditions.

This situation is not unique to the Coachella Valley. More than half of all farmworkers in the country migrate to find work, and most have a hard time finding decent housing, says Moises Loza, executive director of the Housing Assistance Council, a Washington, D.C., nonprofit organization that helps rural organizations develop affordable housing.

"The only difference between the people you see in Mecca [a Coachella Valley village] and the homeless in Los Angeles or San Francisco is that people in Mecca have jobs," says Jeff Hays, director of the Desert Alliance for Community Empowerment in Coachella. "About 40 percent of the migrants in this area you see in vacant lots or garages or clustered together in the trees by canals. The worst off are camping in trees, in boxes, down in Mecca."

Throughout the country, demand for farmworker housing far outpaces supply and funds are desperately short.

A very tough job

Developing affordable housing is difficult in rural areas where density and noise are anathema, infrastructure is underdeveloped, politics are conservative, and local prejudices may center on farmworkers. And there is little economic incentive to build migrant housing. Migrants can pay very little rent, and they move with the seasons.

"Nobody can build housing for people making $5 or $6 per hour who don't work 12 months a year," says John Mealey, executive director of the Coachella Valley Housing Coalition. "We'll never solve the problem unless ag pays more or the federal government and state governments come in and take a big swing at the problem."

Many farmworkers are illegal immigrants, and that complicates matters. USDA-RD requires housing providers to check the immigration status of tenants. "Many migrant workers are illegal, so right off the bat it's hard to use federal money," says Heriberto Rosales, a grant and program specialist with the Rural Community Assistance Corporation, which provides technical assistance and financial support to rural affordable housing providers in 12 Western states. "I haven't heard a story of a successful use of federal funds to house migrant workers considered illegal."

Also, state enforcement of housing standards is a double-edged sword, attacking the hideous conditions often found in farm labor camps but leading many growers to stop providing housing to migrant workers.

"Growers have a very strong interest in finding and securing farmworker housing," says Jasper Hempel, executive vice-president and general counsel for the Western Growers Association, a farmers group in California. "The principal barrier is California's ultra-stringent farmworker housing law. For example, you have to have a window in the bathroom. Even a hotel wouldn't meet that requirement."

The Housing Assistance Council reports that more than half of migrant housing units are crowded; nearly a quarter have serious structural problems; 17 percent of the units are "severely substandard" and 16 percent "moderately substandard." Farmworkers' median household income is $860 per month.

The worst housing in America?

The U.S. Department of Labor stopped calculating the number of farmworkers in the country after reporting a population of 1.6 million in 1995. Roughly 77 percent of that population was born in Mexico and another four percent in other foreign countries.

According to the department, migrants make up roughly 56 percent of the agricultural workforce, but breaking down the population into migrants and home-based workers isn't easy. Many farmworkers are seasonally employed even when they work close to home. These workers often migrate for one or two months a year, leaving families behind.

Most migrants follow one of three main migrant routes. The most popular brings workers from the Southwest and Mexico up through California, Oregon, and Washington. The central stream flows from Texas and Mexico into Rocky Mountain States and the Midwest. The eastern trail starts in Florida and the Caribbean and winds up in New England and upstate New York. Migrants are most often found in seasonal, labor-intensive crops: fruits and row crops. Seasons can vary from a few weeks to six months or longer.

Farmworkers are poor. "In 1999, the median personal income of a farmworker was between $5,000 and $7,500, unchanged since 1988," states a study by Rural Opportunities Inc. in New York. "Farmworkers are becoming poorer because their incomes are stagnant in the face of slowly but steadily rising prices."

Agricultural employees also contend with "the worst housing conditions of any population in the country," says John Henneberger, co-director of the Texas Low-Income Housing Information Service, a statewide advocacy group. "We happened to visit a grower run development outside the city of Muleshoe. It was in the upper 90s. The development hadn't had water for 24 hours. Twenty units of migrant housing were occupied. Residents had to use communal bathrooms and there was no potable water."

Florida provides a snapshot of the housing shortage. "Statewide demand for farmworker housing consists of 96,085 farmworker households with 176,348 household members," says the Florida Housing Finance Corporation. State-licensed labor camps and publicly financed farmworker housing can accommodate 59,330 farmworkers and their family members.

Unaccompanied males are often the hardest to house. Many end up living in camps on growers' land or in overcrowded apartments or trailers. "Relatively few federally subsidized housing units are available for single-male farmworkers," according to a 2002 University of Florida paper prepared for the Miami-Dade Planning and Zoning Department.

With old-fashioned grower-provided camp housing in decline and only a few states investing in farmworker housing, the federal government is frequently the funding source of choice. HUD provides support through Community Development Block Grants, the Rural Housing and Economic Development initiative, and other programs that channel money and expertise through local governments, redevelopment agencies, and housing authorities. It also supports the Housing Assistance Council's Self-Help Homeownership Program and is helping to build regional and national networks of farmworker housing providers and advocates.

USDA-RD has provided grants and loans for about 860 developments with 14,000 units since 1968. The agency funds development and rehabilitation and offers rent subsidies. In FY 2003, USDA-RD offered $37.4 million in loans and $18 million in grant funds for construction of farmworker housing through its section 514 loan and section 516 grant programs. The proposed FY 2004 budget includes $42 million in loans and $17 million in grants.

"Property owners have to jump through a lot of hoops to work with our program," says Art Garcia, housing services administrator for USDA-RD. Staff in USDA-RD's 1,000 state and county offices monitor programs, make sure quality considerations are met, permits are secured, and inspections are conducted.

"Our staff is there on a daily basis, watching the hammering of the nails," Garcia says. He praises the developers USDA-RD relies on to build farmworker housing, saying their work is beautiful. "There's a certain quality; they're built to last," he says.

Down in the valley

Coachella Valley is located in the heart of the Mojave Desert, where summer temperatures reach well into triple digits and rain is rare. Yet farmers have prospered growing dates and table grapes. Growers employ seasonal workers—local people who work as many as 10 months of the year in the fields—and migrants who work the April to August peak seasons.

Figure 1-6 Las Mañanitas, a new development in Riverside County, California. Source: Coachella Valley Housing Coalition

"We have two different groups—people who live here and single males, maybe traveling in a group, passing through—with two different housing needs," observes John Thurman, principal development specialist with the Riverside County Economic Development Authority. "There is an extreme shortage of both types of housing."

Las Mañanitas "fills up right away," according to John Mealey. "We have to turn away up to 200 people a day during the high season."

Tenants at Las Mañanitas pay $25 a week for a bed. They're required to abide by a strict set of rules, including a ban on alcohol and restrictions on noise. The rules are popular with residents. "Where I stayed before, people would just drink all day," says Jesus Ortiz. "I couldn't sleep. I feel more secure, more safe here."

The first phase of Las Mañanitas was completed in 1999. Built on 10 acres owned by EDA and leased at no cost to the Coachella Valley Housing Coalition, Las Mañanitas I contains 11 multi-tenant units with a total of 88 beds, a manager's unit and office, laundry facility, and common areas and outdoor cooking areas. Each furnished unit contains four two-person bedrooms built around a living room, dining room, and kitchen. Las Mañanitas II was completed in December 2002. It consists of 40 beds in five similar multi-tenant units and was financed by the county and HUD.

Proper financing was critical to the project's success. "The key was to keep debt service down," says Marvin Contreras, a financial officer with the coalition. "That's how we can afford to charge residents $25 a week. This project has zero debt service." County funds and rent cover operating expenses, which include the property management fees, salaries, office expenses, water and sewer costs, utilities, and insurance.

Keeping a lid on costs

The Desert Alliance for Community Empowerment (DACE) is developing migrant housing in the nearby village of Oasis. By using polished concrete floors, pre-fabricated panelized housing, and other modest building techniques, DACE hopes to keep costs down to $20,000 or less per bed. That's more than a mobile home would cost, but less than what was spent on Las Mañanitas. "It's a homeless shelter," says Jeff Hays. "We can't have debt."

EDA's ownership of Las Mañanitas meant the development could pass through a streamlined permitting process. "We have a little flexibility," says Thurman. "We don't have to go through variances, conditional-use permits, and zoning requirements."

"The county zoning ordinance doesn't apply to government property," confirms Paul Clark, a Riverside County planner. "Most of the land is in the ag area, which allows for agricultural labor camps, farm buildings, barracks, or migrant agricultural worker mobile homes. Zoning allows these uses so long as they get a conditional-use permit or a plot permit."

Projects the size of Las Mañanitas typically require a public hearing, environmental impact studies, and a more extensive review on the way to a conditional-use permit. DACE's project will require a conditional-use permit, and Hays says the county planning department has "helped substantially on the technical side, saying here's what we need, playing a proactive role."

Innovation and opposition

In the Coachella Valley, housing developers have worked hard to win support for farmworker housing. Clark says elitist opposition to farm-worker housing wouldn't be popular in the current climate, but this isn't always the case.

"We ask people to come to pick crops that are worth millions of dollars, but we don't want them to live in our backyard, we don't want them in our schools; we want them just to come and go," says one HUD housing specialist.

Sister Larraine Lauter, director of Migrant/Immigrant Shelter and Support (M/ISS) in Owensboro, Kentucky, has confronted these problems while developing a hostel for migrant workers. "Looking for land, we met a lot of opposition simply because nobody wanted it next door," says Lauter. "I had people call me and say, 'Sister, do you know what NIMBY means?'"

M/ISS confronted opposition by working to integrate farmworkers into the community, recruiting long-term residents, including local growers, to M/ISS's board, and running programs to orient migrants and new arrivals to the local community. "We never talk about the Hispanic community; we talk about newest members of our community," Lauter says.

Ultimately, M/ISS secured the conditional-use permit needed to develop its hostel, but other housing developers face similar challenges, and many are struggling to come up with innovative solutions. Brien Thane, director of the Office of Rural and Farmworker Housing, a nonprofit in Yakima, Washington, has jumped both financial and planning hurdles. Two years ago, his group developed a 35-unit property that included 18 migrant units. The year-round rentals help cover operating costs, partly subsidizing the migrant units.

"We go to extreme lengths to make sure we get appropriately zoned land," Thane says. "We sometimes need conditional-use permits for community space; sometimes we need to apply for a planned unit development permit to get a better site plan. Usually we try to come in and find a property where we can develop as is."

This strategy has worked elsewhere, too. "We try to design town homes that fit with the zoning," says Howard Porter, executive director of the Alliance for Better Housing in Kennett Square, Pennsylvania. "Unfortunately, there are very few zoning districts or available land that allow multi-family housing or town homes."

"We're looking at purchasing hotels and motels," says John Schmidt, executive director of the New Jersey office of Rural Opportunities, Inc. "That way we don't have to ask for zoning variances. We can rent by the week or by the month; it would almost be like going into the hotel business. It's a commercial venture, which could be financed with a straight mortgage."

Older motels, built before the Interstate system, can be bought inexpensively in many parts of the country, but not in California's Sonoma Valley, a wine-growing region popular with tourists. There, the nonprofit Vineyard Workers Service (VWS) has turned to modular housing as a partial solution to its housing problems.

Last year, VWS received a California Endowment grant through the Rural Community Assistance Corporation for a pilot program linking migrant housing to healthcare. To conform with state and local laws, VWS contracted with a company in neighboring Napa County to build modular units that could be removed from the site (land donated by a local grower) during the off season.

To build on agricultural land, VWS needed building permits, septic permits, temporary power permits, and foundation, plumbing, and fire inspections. The county had to grant an exemption to its prohibition on septic systems. Through contacts with politicians and department heads, Ferris negotiated reduced fees and waivers.

"If you're going to do a project like this, start with the politicians," he says. "Get the county supervisor to buy in and develop relations with the department heads. They understand the spirit of the law."

Sunbelt living

Converted motels, portable modular units, and the trailer homes that are used in many places offer a partial solution to short-term housing needs, particularly in northern areas with short growing and harvest seasons. In other places, attention is being directed to efforts that link migrant housing to long-term housing and community development. After all, farmworkers, including migrants, want more than a bed to sleep in.

"Proximity to shopping and schools, not wanting to travel 30 miles to a grocery store is important to farmworkers," notes Marcus Hepburn, a housing specialist with Florida's Department of Community Affairs.

"We've had a big success in farm-labor housing in Anthony, New Mexico," says USDA's Art Garcia. Located between El Paso and Las Cruces, Anthony produces pecans, onions, and chili, but most farmworkers work at local dairies. They often move up from farmworker housing to adjacent multifamily housing, Garcia says. There is also "self-help" housing, which allows households to build up credit toward a down payment through sweat equity earned by working on their own and neighbors' homes.

The Everglades Community Association (ECA) also offers multi-purpose housing and an array of community services on property it controls in Homestead, Florida. Established in 1982 by farm-labor advocates and growers who had been fighting over control of a county-operated farmworker trailer park, the association became heavily involved in development after Hurricane Andrew wiped out 398 of 400 mobile homes in 1992.

Built with a mix of funds from the USDA, the Federal Home Loan Bank, HUD, and the Florida Home Finance Corporation, housing at ECA serves both migrant and home-based populations. "Everglades Village is a much larger planned community than you would find in a typical tax-abatement project or USDA-funded project," says Steve Kirk, ECA's executive director. "Our planning process was to build more of a self-contained community. When we first planned the village in 1993, we were remote; we needed to include essential services in a master plan."

*Figure 1-7
Heritage Glen in
East Wenatchee
(for families with
50 percent of the
area's median
income). Source:
Office of Rural &
Farmworker
Housing*

Everglades Village currently has 2,250 residents living in 443 units, and additional units are planned. Its town center includes a leasing office, a 6,000-square-foot community center, a social service center, 10,000 square feet in rentable space, and land set aside for education and parks. Retail space will eventually contain a grocery, credit union, computer lab, cafe, and social services. A park was created that is shared with the county, and a parcel has been set aside for a health center.

In response to tenant requests, the project is gated between 6 p.m. and 6 a.m., and security patrols roam the village at night. "I didn't like this from a planning perspective, but people wanted it," says Kirk. "We also have some traditional neighborhood elements. You need a car to go to work, but basic things can be done on site. We have postal boxes in the neighborhood service center, which brings people to the community center on a daily basis."

The village has curbs, gutters, sidewalks, and other details that were not required by law. Although private, the roads and streets were built to local standards. Homes were built close to sidewalks and have front and rear porches. Front yard parking was allowed so residents could keep an eye on their cars. Casa Cesar Chavez, the planned migrant housing, will contain four town houses with seven two- and four-bedroom units. The units will be built later this year (to replace existing trailers) around an enclosed outdoor common space that will be accessed via a key card.

ECA has incorporated some of these design elements into smaller migrant housing projects it's putting up in other parts of Florida. One of these, in Ruskin, will contain 128 beds and is one of three backed by a pilot USDA-funded program.

Hepburn says the project is being developed to house adults traveling alone, but what if demand shifts to family housing? "We wanted flexible design," says Hepburn. "So we came up with quadplexes. The dominant population now will be single adults, but the units can also accommodate families. They're adaptable to possible changes in the population."

Housing grows in wine country

Florida is one of a handful of states whose state government is actively providing farmworker housing or financing. Washington State has given priority to farmworker housing for about five years, increasing funding for agricultural housing and creating a new state-level operating and maintenance fund to help support migrant housing and other special-needs housing. That fund is financed by a $10 surcharge on documents recorded with county assessors.

California operates a pair of programs aimed at housing farmworkers. The Office of Migrant Affairs has built and supports 21 migrant centers throughout the state. These shelter migrant families for up to six months and frequently provide additional services like healthcare or childcare. Most of the centers have been rehabilitated in recent years or are scheduled for rehabilitation, and most are full.

California's other state program, the Joe Serna Farmworker Housing Program, supports farmworker housing development. These programs received a boost in 2000, when the legislature appropriated $55 million for farmworker housing, and again in 2002, when voters approved Proposition 46, an affordable housing bond measure that included an additional $22 million for farmworker housing.

"This was a huge shot in the arm," says Matthew O. Franklin, director of the state's Housing and Community Development department. Serna funds are being used to develop housing for unaccompanied migrants, but many of the priorities are being set at the local level.

Napa County recently used $1.5 million in Joe Serna funds to develop housing for migrant workers in the wine industry. Napa, the country's pre-

Figure 1-8
Raspberry Ridge near Burlington (for those with 35 percent). Source: Office of
Rural & Farmworker Housing

mier wine-producing region, is one of the most successful agrarian economies in the U.S. It's also home to some of the most expensive real estate on
the planet. Increasingly, grape growers rely on a permanent workforce, but
migrants continue to pour into the valley during the growing and harvest
seasons, and the county estimates it will need 300 more beds for migrants
over the next five years.

For several years, donations from the Napa Valley Wine Auction and a
voluntary assessment imposed on growers helped fund camps operated
by the Napa Valley Housing Authority, but more work was needed.

"In 1999, there was a crisis at the Calistoga camp," says Tom Shelton,
CEO of Joseph Phelps Vineyards. "They had 40 guys sleeping in tents with
nowhere to go." Responding to the crisis, the Napa Valley Vintners Association pledged to support a mandatory assessment on vineyards and to
seek volunteers to donate land.

Three things quickly happened: Joseph Phelps offered 10 acres of his
River Ranch land for migrant housing; landowners approved a $10 per
acre assessment on vineyards to support migrant housing; and voters
amended the county general plan, allowing the subdivision of agricultural preserve land for migrant housing.

The assessment (which housing authority director Peter Dreier says will generate $380,000 this year) will be used to operate county-run migrant housing. It freed Napa Valley Wine Auction funds that were previously used to offset the operating deficit to help build new facilities for migrants and affordable housing in the cities as well. Already, the association has redirected $677,000 from the Napa Valley Wine Auction to construction costs at River Ranch, which supplemented the state money and $1.2 million from the county housing trust fund.

Construction of the 60-bed River Ranch project has already been completed, and the facility is occupied. Built of rammed earth by specialist builder David Easton and designed by Don Brandenburger, an architect with wine country experience, the facility is "very efficient and fits with the surroundings," says Shelton.

Vintners and the county are now looking at potential sites for the county's next migrant center. "Realistically, our progress depends on the availability of developable land," Dreier says. "Going through the design approval process could take three to six years, but we're optimistic."

Napa is more affluent and liberal than many rural communities, and it's in a state that provides resources for migrant housing. Its experience is unlikely to be duplicated in many places. Still, it provides an example of what can be done when resources are pooled and the community committed.

The late James Goodno wrote about planning and social justice. His father was a farmworker in Connecticut's tobacco fields as a child. This article was published in November 2003.

Resources
On the web. Housing Assistance Council: www.ruralhome.org. U.S. Department of Agriculture-Rural Development: www.rurdev.usda.gov. Rural Community Assistance Corporation: www.rcac.org. Rural Opportunities: www.ruralinc.org. California Department of Housing and Community Development: www.hcd.ca.gov. Coachella Valley Housing Coalition: www.cvhc.org. Florida Housing Finance Corporation: www.floridahousing.org. Office of Rural and Farmworker Housing: www.orfh.org.

SHADOW KIDS

Homeless youth are not simply younger versions of homeless adults.

By Meghan Stromberg

According to Tim King's last count, taken at 3 a.m. on March 31 this year, 125 young people were sleeping outside in Daley Plaza. They had built shelters from the rain using what they had on hand, mostly sections of wooden pallets and pieces of cardboard. Some were lucky enough to have sleeping bags. And fortunately for all of them, it was a warmer than usual spring night in Chicago—the temperature was in the 40s.

Earlier that day, King—cochair of the Youth Homelessness Team of the local youth advocacy group, Public Action for Change Today—and five other representatives had requested a meeting with Mayor Richard M. Daley to discuss their concerns about homeless youth. Nearly 200 supporters rallied outside in the plaza named for the current leader's father, longtime Chicago mayor Richard J. Daley. When the meeting was denied—for the fourth time since December, King notes—the young people set up camp and slept outside in protest.

Among other things, the group sought full funding of the mayor's 10-Year Plan to End Homelessness, a pilot program to make transit passes available to homeless young people, passage of a set-aside ordinance for new housing, and funding directed specifically at homeless youth programs.

The young people in Chicago expressed a common frustration felt by homeless teens (and the people who look out for them): Homeless young people are different from the adult homeless population and they tend to get overlooked.

"Homeless people in general, and kids in particular, really do slip through the cracks," says Melissa Maguire, director of the Youth Shelter Network of the nonprofit, nondenominational Chicago organization, The Night Ministry, which serves homeless and low-income youth and adults in a variety of ways. "And, they've got those same developmental issues as [teens] who aren't homeless, but for them there's no safety net [of parental support]," she adds.

A boy named Aaron

For some of the young people camping in Daley Plaza this past March, sleeping out in public or in an unsafe place was a familiar experience. King's cochair at PACT, Aaron Bowen, became homeless in the fall of 2004 at age 19. Now 21, Bowen is employed and plans to attend the University of Chicago in the fall. He currently lives in a single-room-occupancy apartment, provided through the nonprofit Heartland Alliance for Human Needs and Human Rights.

The short version of the story goes like this: Bowen moved in with his mother after returning from college, but they couldn't overcome "issues of his lifestyle," he says. Bowen, who refers to himself as queer, was physically abused and finally kicked out of the house.

He, like many homeless teens, "couch-surfed," staying for a few nights or weeks with a friend or relative, but maintaining friendships was hard and eventually impossible. "My friends couldn't take care of me," Bowen says. They also couldn't relate to him or his situation.

People on the streets weren't any more helpful. Bowen stayed with acquaintances, many of whom would toss him out when he didn't pay his way—with sex—after a few days. One employer let him stay for a week or two before sexually assaulting him and robbing him of his savings account and all his personal possessions.

He became resourceful—sleeping on trains, showering at the gym, and walking dogs to make money. But the good-looking young man says he got little sympathy from other street people, and was told again and again, "Why don't you just go be an escort?"

"I've studied abroad, got into Yale," Bowen says. He never figured he'd have to trade his body for food or shelter. "I was taken advantage of by a lot of people," he says. "It was very, very painful."

Teenage wasteland

Bowen's story is not unique. Homeless teens, properly referred to as unaccompanied homeless youth, are an extremely vulnerable group. More than half of them report being "beaten up" while on the streets, according to the National Alliance to End Homelessness, and the rates of sexual assault of homeless youth range from 15 to 20 percent. Homeless youth and youth service providers report that adult homeless shelters are among the most dangerous places to be.

Contrary to popular belief, homeless youth workers say, kids who run away and become homeless aren't bad kids who just want to rebel. "There's a perception that homeless youth enjoy living in the streets without rules," says Ken Cowdery, executive director of New Avenues for Youth in Portland, Oregon. "The vast majority of kids we deal with are victims of severe abuse—'smart' runaways escaping dangerous situations."

A 2003 study by the Center for Law and Social Policy found that half of the homeless youth interviewed reported "intense conflict or physical harm by a family member." Other studies back that up. "Wherever I Can Lay My

Head: Homeless Youth on Homelessness," a 2005 study issued by Chicago's Department of Children and Youth Services and The Night Ministry, reports that instances of emotional or physical abuse by family members were greater than 50 percent. It also found that 36 percent of homeless girls and almost 14 percent of boys were sexually abused at home.

Experts point out that many homeless kids don't run away at all. As opposed to runaways, "throwaways" are kids who have been kicked out of the house, slowly driven out, or abandoned by their parents. The CLASP study found that 62 percent of the homeless youth interviewed said that a member of their family or household had let them know they were no longer wanted.

The reasons kids find themselves homeless and alone are many. Like Aaron Bowen, lots of teenagers end up on the street because of familial conflict concerning sexual orientation. In the Chicago study, 13.5 percent cited sexual orientation as a factor that led to homelessness. One 17-year-old transgender youth quoted in the study reveals just how stark family life for a LGBTQ (lesbian, gay, bisexual, transgender, questioning) youth can be: "[My] parents moved away without me."

Many other conflicts that contribute to homelessness have to do with teen pregnancy or parenting—11 percent and six percent, respectively, according to the study. Drug and alcohol abuse—both by teens and their parents—is also frequently a contributing factor to youth homelessness, as are issues of mental health.

A family history of homelessness, unstable housing, or economic crises may also lead to youth homelessness. A 2004 U.S. Conference of Mayors study of 27 major cities found that families with children accounted for 50 percent of the urban homeless population, and that population is thought to be larger in rural areas. The study noted that while shelter capacity for families increased in 2004, about one-third of requests for shelter were denied that year. Complicating matters for teens, particularly boys, is that finding shelter often means splitting up the family. Men and boys (sometimes as young as 10) are frequently not allowed in shelters that also serve women and children.

Other homeless youth come out of the foster care system, having either run away from foster parents and group homes or having "aged out" (generally at age 18, but at 21 in some states) from the system. Minors who haven't been emancipated can receive substantial help only from within the child welfare system—the law obliges care providers to report them and turn them over.

Still others are kids released from the juvenile justice system who refuse to go home or don't have a family to go back to. The list goes on.

The hidden homeless

Although counts vary and are difficult to obtain, the National Runaway Switchboard's figure—1.3 to 2.8 million unaccompanied homeless youth and runaways in the U.S.—generally hits the range other groups report. Compare that number with the 60 million young people aged 10 to 24 counted in the 2000 Census, and the homeless represent two to five percent of the total.

The high numbers of young people on the street, ranging in age from preteens to early twenties, surprised this reporter. Working and living in Chicago, I frequently see men on the streets, particularly older men, and some single women and women with young kids. I don't notice teens. "The reason they're not seen is because they don't want to be," says The Night Ministry's Maguire. "They want to be hidden because they don't want to be victimized" or further marginalized, she says.

She tells me about one girl who couch-surfed at various friends' and relatives' homes for a year in order to finish high school—and no one at school knew her secret. (She showed up at the shelter only when she became pregnant.) Homeless kids try to blend in by wearing the same clothes as other kids and hanging out near colleges and other places frequented by young people. "Peer pressure at that age strongly contributes to the desire to blend in," Maguire points out.

Homeless youth are considered a hard-to-serve population because of their relative invisibility compared with other homeless groups. They have also been let down time and again in their young lives, and as a consequence, they can be extremely wary of others, particularly adults. On the other hand, experts say, they tend to be tremendously resilient and often very positive. In a way, their comfort with disappointment and low expectations may keep them from getting discouraged too soon.

Legal limbo

Homeless teens are also invisible in legal terms. Kids under the age of 18 have little legal autonomy, and those 18 and older may no longer qualify for social programs aimed at children—such as foster care—that they may have depended on for years (although the foster care system does provide some after-care support).

The National Law Center on Homelessness and Poverty publishes a booklet aimed at unaccompanied homeless youth under age 18 that explains homeless teens' legal rights. One of the first questions in the Q & A-format handout asks if minors can stay in housing provided through the federal Runaway and Homeless Youth Act without a parent or guardian. The answer captures a paradox: "Yes, but the law requires the program to contact the youth's family within 72 hours of the youth entering the shelter."

Unaccompanied youth may receive food stamps without parental consent. If they are disabled, some may access Supplemental Security Income, and if they are at least 16, they can do so without consent. They also have the right to attend school, and the federal McKinney-Vento Act, passed in 1987, guarantees various specific education-related rights. Pregnant homeless teens and teens with children may qualify for Temporary Assistance for Needy Families, but only if they live in an approved living situation (one of which, interestingly, is "with a parent or legal guardian"). Typically, homeless youth don't qualify for public housing unless they have kids of their own.

Some services, such as job training programs, require a parent's signature, while others do not. The NLCHP booklet is 28 pages long—an indication of the legal complexities unaccompanied homeless youth face. Social workers, however, are skilled in helping unaccompanied youth navigate their rights.

Without a home

At the root of teen homelessness, just as it is for adults and families, is a chronic, well-documented affordable housing shortage. (A March 2006 study of rental housing by the Joint Center for Housing Studies and Harvard University added to the volume of literature on the topic. It found that although 100,000 affordable rental units were built in the U.S. every year, 200,000 were torn down.)

"[Youth] have the additional barrier of not being old enough to sign a lease, for instance," explains Nan Roman, president of the National Alliance to End Homelessness. "Issues having to do with their age make it more difficult, but housing affordability is certainly the driver."

In the past, cities, states, and the federal government have largely adopted policies aimed at managing the problem of homelessness. Emergency shelters, food pantries, job training, substance abuse clinics, mental health programs, and other programs sought to help stabilize homeless and at-risk people, on the assumption that a more stable life would make finding and keeping permanent housing more feasible.

That's changing, however. Today's efforts are centered around "housing first," with the idea that only when someone is in a safe, reliable place can they begin to work on other life issues. The housing first model is problematic, however, for unaccompanied young people.

"While we have a clear path for ending homelessness among adults, this path might not be quite as clear for youth," says Roman. "They need housing and they need support. And they often need housing in a different way."

She notes that their general lack of education and experience—with living on their own, engaging in various social situations and with the larger community, and working—makes the needs of teens very different from those of adults. And long-term, so-called "permanent" housing doesn't suit homeless teens as well as it might older homeless individuals. Young people by nature are a fairly mobile group, and it's unrealistic to expect an 18-year-old to want to stay put in one apartment for a year, let alone a decade, Roman notes.

"As in so many realms, we're just not adequately attending to the housing needs of young people who are vulnerable," Roman says.

Where to go?

Homeless kids who seek help are likely to make first contact at a youth shelter or through an outreach program that sends staff and volunteers into the streets to give out food, clothing, and counseling, as well as information on shelters, medical treatment, and other services. At a shelter, staff will first try to reunite a homeless youth with his or her family or a relative—if safe and appropriate—or contact child welfare if the teen is a ward of the state.

Then—if the kid doesn't go back to the streets—they work towards whatever longer-term placement is appropriate, because homeless kids can't stay in a shelter forever.

Indeed, shelter care has its limitations. Under the 1974 federal Runaway and Homeless Youth Act, which helps fund local nonprofits that serve runaway, homeless, missing, and sexually exploited children, basic centers (emergency shelters) offer residential care for up to 15 days, as well as providing meals, clothing, and medical care (or access to such care); counseling; and after-care services. The staffs seek to reunite youth with family—if possible—or find alternative placements with relatives, foster care, or in family-style group homes. While for some, making contact with these shelters may be the first step towards ending homelessness, many drop in for a day or a week before moving on. Then the cycle repeats.

In transition

The idea is to get kids into a normal setting—or at least work toward it. For younger kids, that often means a family-like setting with foster parents or in a group home. For older kids, the best option is often a transitional living program, which helps them acquire the know-how to live self-sufficiently so that they can eventually get and keep permanent housing on their own.

"Normal" for the vast majority of young people just starting out includes relying on financial support from family members, if needed. Parents also help their young adult children look for apartments, negotiate leases, and deal with other unfamiliar tasks. Homeless kids have no such familial support, and that makes finding and keeping conventional housing very difficult.

The transitional living programs that receive funding from RHYA last as long as 18 months (sometimes longer for teens under 18). Living accommodations may vary—from group homes to market-rate apartments—but all programs offer a mix of training in life skills (such as budgeting and parenting), interpersonal skills, and job skills, as well as traditional educational opportunities such as GED programs and alternative high schools. When employment becomes stable, youth are expected to contribute a fixed amount or a percentage of their income towards housing costs.

Figure 1-9
A volunteer helps a young man with his school work at The Night Ministry. Such interactions have a dual purpose: Youth learn about the three Rs as well as how to interact in various social situations.
Source: The Night Ministry

Lighthouse Youth Services in Cincinnati opened its Lighthouse Runaway Shelter (now called the Youth Crisis Center) in 1974, and was one of the first recipients of funding under RHYA and the only youth shelter in the area. Each year, the 24-bed facility serves 1,500 children ages 10 through 17—even if some have to sleep on cots, says Bob Mecum, president and CEO. Lighthouse has had success getting younger teens into foster homes, and eventually, a third of them get adopted, he notes.

Early on, however, Mecum saw a huge gap in care for kids 18 and up. "As we learned more about the adult shelter care facilities, we began to realize how many older youth were going into these adult shelters and really not doing well," Mecum says. "These 18-, 19-, and 20-year-olds were so remarkably different than the older, stereotypical homeless adult with mental health problems, addiction," and chronic homelessness.

"And adult shelters were having a hard time," he adds. "[Young adults] were coming in with behavioral issues—fighting, aggressive behavior,

Figure 1-10
Foundation support allowed The Night Ministry to replace its 12-year-old Health Out-reach Bus with a larger, better equipped one. It visits 10 sites six nights a week, delivering food, medical care, and support to youth and adults. Source: The Night Ministry

neediness. Adult shelters had trouble engaging them and some were being preyed upon by older adults."

In 1989, Lighthouse began operating its Transitional Living Program. Initially, to receive HUD funding, Mecum says, the program had to focus on housing; it placed young adults in buildings that the agency owned—similar to permanent housing solutions for adults. At one point, the agency owned four such apartment buildings where teens would live, with supervision, as they learned independent living skills, finished their education, and learned how to get a job.

Today, the program continues, but with fewer agency-owned buildings. Mecum notes that about 90 youth currently live in leased, scattered-site apartments in the community, thanks in part to a shift in HUD's funding model.

Mecum sees a place for both models, depending on the person. "The most ideal aspect of the scattered-site model," he says, "is that you cannot only put them in a location that makes sense for the person, near work or school, for instance, but also turn the apartment over to them if the person is able to get a job and learn how to keep the apartment. Even as they get older, they don't have to leave."

Matt Schnars likes the scattered site model as well. Schnars, the independent living program director at Haven House Services in Raleigh, North Carolina, works with teens aged 16 to 21; 75 percent of them enter his program at 18 or 19. "Many have been involved with programs [such as Haven House's group foster homes], have been in foster care, the juvenile justice system, or mental health group homes," he says. "They haven't had the support to transition out into the community and they have no idea what it takes to go out and obtain housing. Some are functioning on a 5th or 6th grade reading level—they don't have the skills to get a job or negotiate with a landlord."

Transitional and semi-independent living programs allow young adults to learn those things and put them into practice, while still giving them a safety net. "They may find themselves in totally unfamiliar territory—in middle-class society where the survival skills from their street life don't apply," Schnars says. "Being out of their element, there's a natural fear of failure."

Schnars tells the story of one young woman who called in a panic because she had just gotten paid and didn't know what to do with her check. "She wanted help getting her money put away before she blew it," he says. "They're aware of their vulnerability," he adds.

Two in one

Chicago's Night Ministry handles transitional housing a little differently. It just opened a new facility that accommodates its 120-day interim housing program, which has served about 200 youth ranging in age from 14 to 21 (and their young children) annually since opening in 1992.

As its name implies, the interim program is "smack dab in the middle" of the care spectrum, Maguire says. Youth may stay longer than they would in an emergency shelter—and receive the support they need—while they prepare for the next step towards solving their homelessness. At the dorm-style Open Door Shelter, two teens share a room that has been carefully fitted with furniture, rugs, and linens that say "home" rather than "institution." The residents attend school or work during the day and participate in life-skill classes, counseling sessions, job-skill training, and other group and individual activities at night.

The average stay in the four-month program is 30 to 40 days, and Maguire says she sees youth, particularly older youth, come back two and three times. "Would we like them to stay 120 days? Yes. But they get excited and want to fly out on their own."

For those not quite ready to fly, the new facility also offers two transitional living apartments on the top floor, where eight young men and women, and their infants or toddlers, can live for one to two years while practicing independent living skills.

Residents of the apartments each have a case manager who helps them learn the skills to become self-sufficient, but the youth have more autonomy, personal space, and responsibility than residents of the interim program. Maguire expects that some youth who move up to the apartments may realize they're not quite ready yet, and may move back downstairs into the interim program. And that's perfectly O.K.

Keeping tabs

The Homeless Youth System in Portland, Oregon, is often cited for its efficiency, effectiveness, and level of collaboration with other homeless service providers, mental and physical health professionals, and even the police. (When cops pick up teens for minor offenses, they're not taken to a juvenile detention center but to the reception center, which gets in touch with the family and offers counseling and access to other services.)

Together, three organizations—New Avenues for Youth, Janus Youth Programs, and Outside In—operate an intake center, shelters, day services centers (for meals, showers, storage facilities), drug and alcohol treatment programs, an alternative high school, a medical clinic, and transitional and independent housing.

The youth system is also part of a sophisticated data management system. New Avenues for Youth's Ken Cowdery says that people come from all over the country, as well as places such as Mexico, New Zealand, and China, asking, "How did you do this?" "I tell them this," Cowdery says. "People were frustrated with the lack of coordination. Add to that a great deal of compassion and a lot of smart people in government who know how to get things done and who knew it was important to have a unified database."

That database not only gives New Avenues easy-to-use data, but it also provides reliable information to governments and private donors, as well as to the media (which is credited in Portland for having helped to publicize and demand action on the city's homelessness problems).

All agencies collect data about the people they serve, but, says Heather Lyons, homeless program manager for the Portland Bureau of Housing and Development, Portland's model is different because it allows various service providers to share information. It opens up the silos of service to create a more collaborative atmosphere of care. The system-wide Homeless Managemanent Information System is being implemented, in part, in response to a 2004 congressional mandate that recipients of HUD's Continuum of Care homelessness funds participate in an HMIS.

"But ours goes beyond the federal mandate, touching services for low-income or at-risk populations, people with chemical dependence problems," and other groups that aren't necessarily—but may be—homeless, Lyons notes. (Congress has also laid out a plan to better track kids exiting the foster care system, but the Youth in Transition Database hasn't yet been implemented.)

Homeward bound

One formerly homeless young woman in Portland offered her gratitude in a letter to New Avenues for Youth. "I know that when I'm older and when my life is more stabel [sic] my time will be a more appropriate way of showing my thanks," she wrote. "For now my words are all I have to give."

Because of the various programs and people looking out for them, she and a lot of other teens across the U.S. will lay down their heads tonight—and the next night—in a safe place. It may not be what most people envision when they think of home, but it might be better than the car, abandoned building, lumpy couch of a friend of a friend, or highway underpass that these youths may have called "home" shortly before.

For Aaron Bowen, who's living in an SRO in Chicago, working, and heading up PACT's homeless team, things are definitely looking up, but not altogether rosy. "I got robbed last Wednesday," he told me when we talked in early April.

But the young man, who says he has been a youth advocate since he was 15, feels passionately about his role and that of other formerly homeless youth in combating youth homelessness—which is why he shares his story.

Meghan Stromberg is *Planning's* senior editor. This article was published in June 2006.

Resources

Online. APA's Policy Guide on Homelessness is available at www.planning.org/policyguides. The Center for Law and Social Policy: www.clasp.org; Haven House Services: www.havenhousenc.org; Lighthouse Youth Services: www.lys.org. The website of the National Alliance to End Homelessness is at www.endhomelessness.org.

More. National Runaway Switchboard: www.nrscrisisline.org; New Avenues for Youth: www.newavenues.org; The Night Ministry: www.thenightministry.org. "The Survival Guide to Homelessness," a blog written by a formerly homeless man in California, is available at http://guide2homelessness.blogspot.com.

LEARNING FROM THE HOMELESS

By Ruth Eckdish Knack, AICP

As the regional homeless coordinator for the Southern Nevada Region Planning Coalition, Shannon West has heard plenty about the multiple causes of homelessness—often from the down and out themselves.

What it all boils down to, she says, is the lack of housing. "To end homelessness, you need housing. That's clear."

Las Vegas has made the news in the last few years for its rather blunt attempts to deal with the homeless problem. It has tried to close encampments, make some parks off-limits, and outlaw "mobile soup kitchens." It's time to try something else, says West.

The daughter of an Air Force officer, West grew up "everywhere," including Las Vegas, where she spent part of her elementary school years. At Florida State University, where she majored in political science but was not, she says, a great student, she worked at a runaway shelter in Tallahassee—the first one in the city.

She put that experience to work when she came back to Las Vegas after graduation and found work in a nonprofit residential treatment center for runaways. Later, she earned a master's degree in social work from the University of Nevada, Las Vegas. (She's now working on a Ph.D. in public policy.)

In 1994, West started working in a Clark County antiviolence program. That led to a job managing a neighborhood justice center and later to one as assistant director of the Clark County parks and recreation department.

"All that is what prepared me for this job," she says. "I'm a social worker by discipline, but my work experience gave me an understanding of the need to balance various issues."

Today that translates into serving the needs of the homeless while recognizing the public's desire for safe and peaceful neighborhoods.

In the last few years, says West, "there has been a major focus on ending homelessness in southern Nevada." So when the county manager asked her to consider a new position as homeless coordinator, she was inclined to give it a try.

Turnaround

The Southern Nevada Regional Planning Coalition has been around for years as a technical working group, West says. But it dealt with more typical planning issues: transportation, housing, the environment. With the formation of the Committee on Homelessness and the creation of the coordinator position, the coalition broadened its focus.

The homelessness committee, which was initiated by Las Vegas Mayor Oscar Goodman, includes representatives of the county and its four municipalities along with representatives of agencies that deal with the homeless: mental health, the Veterans Administration, and various community organizations.

The coalition conducts a biennial homeless census, organizes a management information system, and runs several shelters. The jurisdictions involved pay into a fund that now totals some $44 million, including $4.4 million for regional planning and shelters. The shelters house some 11,000 homeless people on any given day, says West. About 50,000 a year are referred to various services offered by the coalition.

Is that figure as large as it seems to some community residents and visitors? "No, I don't think it is disproportionately large" for the size of the area, says West, although she admits that in raw numbers Las Vegas has "the honor" of having the nation's largest number of homeless people. But with a limited geographic area, she says, it's hard to compare with other cities, "so the numbers may not create a fair picture."

Las Vegas does make things harder for the marginally employed, she notes. "There's simply not enough affordable housing here even for people with moderate incomes—teachers, for instance. They end up living in low-income housing, which means not much is left for the really poor."

West's first task as coordinator was to carry out a census of the homeless population. The result of last July's count is a 300-page study that shows 21 percent of this population is "chronically homeless," including many who are physically or mentally disabled.

The surprising figure, she says, is the 73 percent that are considered transitional, or short-time, homeless. They have been homeless for less than a year, often because they suffered some trauma.

Asked whether there is a link with gambling (an obvious question in Las Vegas), she responds that "studies show some intersection but not one of major causality." Instead, the most frequent cause is loss of a job. The second is addiction either to drugs or alcohol.

West is quite proud of the comprehensiveness of the homeless survey. "We can be sure of the results because we use a solid methodology to gather our baseline data," she says. In addition, homeless "guides" are hired to seek out respondents for peer-to-peer surveys in shelters and on the streets.

With the accurate baseline data, the coalition will be able to compare results in 2009. Already, says West, there is some progress to report.

The most significant item is the coalition's regional plan to end homelessness, which West refers to as a business case. "We wanted to paint a picture that potential investors—public and private—could understand," she says. The committee on homelessness has established a trust fund for contributors, who include casinos operators.

The 10-point plan is based on three major strategies, summed up in the title, Help, Hope, and Home:

• Help—Planning for outcomes (build an infrastructure to deliver services).

• Hope—Prevention (stop homelessness before it starts).

• Home—Focus on housing (and quickly rehouse people who become homeless).

The first strategy, planning for outcomes, requires a clear roadmap for change, West says. The focus on prevention means, among other things, understanding the intersection between child welfare and homelessness.

The key to the program is the third strategy, which depends on a supply of affordable permanent housing, along with services such as rental assistance and working with the institutions, including schools and health care, that will keep the formerly homeless on track.

West stresses the need not to give up on those who repeatedly fall into homelessness. "If that happens, we have to move them back into housing quickly and provide drug and alcohol rehab, mental health, and job services," she says.

Meanwhile, West and her staff are working on several initiatives. One is to convince homeless people who live in encampments throughout the valley to move to shelters. "We have a clear set of protocols to deal with this community," she says. "When we find an encampment, we send social workers out to offer help." The results have been good. Over the last 20 months, about half the encampments that the group has worked with have agreed to move inside.

"That's a big deal," she says, citing the example of a parcel of land owned by the Bureau of Land Management that the county wanted to lease for flood control and that the BLM wanted to preserve to save a rare buckwheat species. Twenty-one of the 25 homeless people agreed to leave for shelters, thanks to the staff's efforts.

In November 2007, the coalition held its first Project Homeless Connect outreach event, modeled after a similar daylong event held in San Francisco. "It's a one-stop shop, where the homeless can go to get everything," she says. Over 2,600 homeless people came through the door that day.

For those who doubt the value of programs like hers, West suggests looking at the costs of homelessness, which are documented in her study. "You will be astonished," she says. "It costs $50,000 a year to live on the streets. That's compared with $11,000 a year to put someone in housing with services."

Ruth Knack is *Planning's* executive editor. This article was published in February 2008.

2

Special Needs

Most Americans have choices when picking a place to live. They make decisions based on affordability or proximity to work, school, or family. But some Americans have little or no choice about where to live.

Elderly people without cars have more limited housing choices than drivers do. The carless elderly may find it difficult to remain in their homes unless they can rely on someone who drives an automobile or their communities offer good transportation systems. According to the National Institute on Aging, about 600,000 people aged 70 or older stop driving every year.

Many families who are displaced from public housing units must scramble to find housing because subsidized replacement units are scarce and may take years to build.

Housing is a question mark for others as well, including refugees who are new to the U.S. and sex offenders who are looking for housing. Refugees have the advantage of federal sponsorship, but the job of easing their assimilation falls to local communities, which must supply appropriate housing and services. Sex offenders are stigmatized by law. Nearly two dozen states and hundreds of municipalities have passed laws restricting where convicted sex offenders may live after leaving prison. The Georgia supreme court ruled in November 2007 that the state's residency restriction law was invalid.

Figure 2-1
The Senior Wheels program in Appleton, Wisconsin, provides demand-respon-
sive transportation for seniors. Volunteer drivers use their own vehicles.
Source: Holly Keenan, Making the Ride Happen

GROWING OLD IN A CAR-CENTRIC WORLD

Americans love their automobiles. What does that mean for an aging nation?

By Meghan Stromberg

My grandmother, Margie Thomas, is 80 years old and widowed. She has lived on the same land in southeastern Iowa for 62 years. Before that she lived 10 miles down the road. Her house was paid off long ago, and a portion of her income comes from payments she receives from the Department of Agriculture to keep her farmland out of production.

Thomas is one of many older rural Americans who depend on their cars. Her house is two miles from the nearest paved road and from the closest town, What Cheer, which shrank from a population of 1,400 in 1940 to 678 in 2000, and has lost most of its stores, restaurants, and churches along the way.

The grocery store, pharmacy, and Wal-Mart—her three top destinations, which she tends to tackle all at once—are 20 miles away. A couple of times a month she travels 30 miles to see her doctors. She doesn't make many social visits. Yet, even with so few trips, she keeps two cars in case one breaks down.

What will happen when she must hang up her car keys? "Won't you come take care of me?" she jokes. She says she may have to move to a bigger town or relocate to northern Illinois, where her daughter lives. She doesn't even consider staying put.

More and more Americans are getting to be just like Margie Thomas. Some 39.9 million people (12 percent of the total U.S. population) were over age 65 in 2000, and of those, 12.3 million were over 75. The Census Bureau projects that 71.4 million people (almost 20 percent of the total population) will be 65 or older in 2030.

Two decades from now, seniors will account for a quarter of all drivers. Older drivers tend to have lower accident rates than other drivers but also slower reaction times and more physical problems. However, not every senior will be behind the wheel.

Maintaining mobility for older Americans is already a huge challenge, and it's going to get more difficult. The oldest baby boomers turn 61 this year, and while most of them drive, will they have enough transportation options when they choose not to drive, or are unable to?

To drive or not to drive?

While environmentalists and others tout the benefits of a car-free lifestyle, people who are involuntarily carless can feel quite isolated.

That's especially true in rural areas and suburbs—which are, coincidentally, where an increasing number of older Americans live. That's partly because people are choosing to age in place. At the same time, young people are leaving their rural towns. Taken together, those factors help to explain why Maine and Wyoming are projected to be second and third (behind Florida) in the Census Bureau's ranking of states by percentage of residents over age 65 in 2030, even as they rank among the least populated, at 32nd and 44th, respectively.

Today, one in five older people does not drive. Personal preference is one reason why, but there are other reasons as well: Some have no access to a car, or they're prevented from driving because of a physical impairment, or they self-regulate—choosing not to drive out of concern for their own safety.

In a recent survey in northern Virginia, 42 percent of respondents age 75 and older indicated that they had not driven in the past week because of general physical problems. One in five said they were not confident about driving due to slow reaction times, and another 18 percent had vision problems. Frequency of driving tends to decline after people reach age 75, says Jane Hardin, coordinator of the senior transportation program of the Community Transportation Association of America, but age isn't a decisive factor. Health, lifestyle, and location play a bigger role. "An older person often keeps the car and uses it where he's comfortable," she says.

Are we there yet?

Elinor Ginzler, director of AARP's Livable Communities program, points to the "sheer weight of this demographic wave" of aging baby boomers—those born between 1946 and 1964—as either a challenge or window of opportunity for planners. "We have to ask ourselves: Are we doing what we can?" Ginzler says.

By at least one account, the answer is: not really. "It's a classic example of a problem you could see coming, and for whatever reason, government, businesses, and individuals haven't planned for it," says Joe Coughlin, director of the AgeLab at MIT, a multidisciplinary, government- and business-funded research program focused on older Americans.

In a nationwide online poll of 378 metropolitan planning organizations, the New England University Transportation Center (which Coughlin heads) and the AgeLab asked whether the organizations were prepared to meet the needs of older people. Fifty-six percent indicated that current transportation services were inadequate, and 68 percent said that the needs of baby boomers will require a fundamentally different transportation system. Only 11 percent agreed that their region is adequately funding infrastructure, vehicles, and services to meet the needs of aging baby boomers 20 years from now.

The good news is that almost a third of the MPOs have developed a specific plan estimating the needs of future boomers, and 18 percent already have projects under way to meet those needs. "The planning has got to be done," Coughlin says. "As a baby boomer myself, I'm hoping we'll get the job done by the time I need it."

The 'longevity paradox'

Coughlin says we are facing a "longevity paradox." In 1900, the average life expectancy was 47. Today, people can live 40 or even 50 years beyond that. "Humanity's greatest success is also our greatest challenge," he says. "We are living longer and better, in terms of health, but we have not built the physical infrastructure to envision how we would live, work, play, and move."

*Figure 2-2
In Chicago and other big cities, many older people walk to get places.
Source: Meghan Stromberg*

"It took 60 years to get the urban form and land uses that are in place today—even doubling the pace of change wouldn't get us there fast enough," he says. Besides, it doesn't appear that we are about to abandon our spread-out land-use patterns any time soon.

For Americans, cars are a sign of independence. That is particularly true for baby boomers, says Bobbie Beson-Crone, the manager of the Wisconsin Department of Transportation's Human Services Transportation Coordination program. In comparison to previous generations, "both men and women were raised to be independent," she says. "We all come from two-car families."

And while boomers may see signs that they are getting older, how many of them picture themselves living without a car? "Driving is so much a part of the American identity," Coughlin says. "Not being able to drive is not just giving up a certain mobility mode, but also changing how we define independence and freedom."

Stuck at home

Many people who don't drive are either homebound or go out only to visit the doctor and grocery store. According to AARP, whose 39 million members are age 50 and older, remaining active is a key component of "successful aging," defined as the ability to make choices, have a positive influence on others, and be involved in the world. A third of all older non-drivers report "frequently feeling isolated from other people," compared to 19 percent of drivers.

How often someone stays at home is a common measure of social isolation in senior research. According to "Aging Americans: Stranded Without Options," a 2004 study from the Surface Transportation Policy Partnership and AARP, half of all nondrivers age 65 and over—3.6 million Americans—stay home on any given day because they lack transportation. The report indicates that rural communities and sprawling suburbs, households without a car, and African Americans, Latinos, and Asian Americans are most heavily affected.

Nondrivers over the age of 50 also make less than half as many total trips as drivers of the same age, according to a survey from AARP. That survey, "Beyond 50.05: A Report to the Nation on Livable Communities," indicates that nondrivers are six times more likely to miss out on things they want to do. That means communities and the economy may be losing out, too, by failing to benefit from the potential engagement and buying power of less mobile older people.

If they no longer drive themselves, many seniors "slide over," Ginzler says, becoming a passenger in their own car, or that of a friend or family member or a volunteer. An AARP survey found that 56 percent of nondrivers age 50 to 74 make most of their trips as passengers in a car, while 70 percent of seniors age 75 and up do so. In rural areas in particular, this informal transportation system is often well-established. "The social network becomes unbelievably important there," she says. "It's pretty remarkable how individuals step in to fill gaps."

On foot

One transportation option that urban seniors use regularly is walking. That's true in Northern Virginia, where the ratio of people age 65 and older is expected to go from one in 13 today to one in seven in 2030 and the number of nondriving seniors could double. In that region, walking is the second most used form of transportation after the car (with seniors as drivers or passengers), according to a telephone survey of more than 1,600 households whose residents are 75 or older. The survey was conducted by the Northern Virginia Transportation Commission as part of a larger 2006 report evaluating senior mobility needs.

The survey divided the population by community type: walkable urban, in-town, or mixed use; suburban development with separated residential and retail land uses; and rural-exurban. At 48 percent, the number of seniors in urban locations that reported having walked to a destination in the past week was more than two times greater than those in suburban locations and almost five times more than in rural places.

"People from walkable, mixed use areas reported more trips per week," says Jana Lynott, AICP, formerly a planner with the NVTC and now AARP's strategic policy advisor. "That's a positive outcome of a well-designed community."

Figure 2-3
Margie Thomas's
house in rural Iowa.
Source: Meghan
Stromberg

In various surveys, however, older people cite safety concerns as barriers to walking. Those concerns include a lack of sidewalks or limited sidewalk connectivity, too few crosswalks, high traffic speeds, poor lighting, and fear of crime. The Washington Department of Transportation points out that while the elderly make up 12 percent of the state's population, they represent 17 percent of pedestrian casualties. Seniors are in most danger at intersections—as are all pedestrians—but they also are victims of other types of accidents as well.

A 2004 Hawaii report showed a disproportionate number of fatalities for seniors: More than half of all pedestrian deaths in 2002 involved the elderly, although seniors accounted for only 11 percent of the population. When older walkers were asked about safety, most said that crossing the street is more dangerous than it was 10 years ago and more than half said walk signals are too short.

The trouble with transit

Taking public transportation seems to be a natural choice for people without a car, and in areas where sufficient transit options are available, older people tend to use it, the STPP report says, noting that nondrivers 65 and over made 310 million trips in 2001. But according to Jana Lynott, other evidence suggests that less than two percent of all trips taken by that group are on public transportation.

Public transportation may be good for commuters, but it may not be efficient for medical appointments, shopping, or social visits, or for trips with multiple destinations. "I would never take transit to get to the doctor, but it gets me to work everyday," says AARP's Ginzler, who lives and works in the Washington, D.C., area. "For me to take Metro to get to the doctor's office would take about four times longer than to get there in my car."

Mass transit also focuses primarily on the city as the economic and cultural hub of a region, whereas both workers and nonworkers of all ages often need to get around an outlying area or require suburb-to-suburb transportation.

Finally, fewer than half of all adults live near transit, and a third of Americans over 75 have a medical condition that makes all travel, including standard transit, difficult. Others find that their community may lack adequate sidewalks, crosswalks, bus shelters, signage, lighting, and other features that make taking a bus or train practical and pleasant for an older person. For both groups, complementary paratransit services—demand-responsive bus service that operates within three quarters of a mile of transit stops—can provide access to the local fixed route service.

Transportation authorities are required under the Americans with Disabilities Act to provide paratransit service for the elderly and the disabled. While essential for senior mobility, that service can be expensive and inefficient. Lawrence, Kansas, is a university town that tends to attract retirees because of its walkability, cultural opportunities, medical facilities, and public transportation, says Cliff Galante, the city's transit administrator. But with recent double-digit growth, "the demand for paratransit service sometimes outstrips resources," he notes.

Demand-responsive transportation options that offer door-to-door service—and are run by local nonprofit organizations, aging or health and human service agencies, or transportation agencies—do much of the heavy lifting in outlying areas. Capital funding, but not money for operations, often comes from the federal Elderly and Persons with Disabilities Transportation Program (Section 5310).

But, like paratransit, many of these programs lack the efficiency and funding to be truly cost-effective. Because providers generally have separate funding—and separate regulations regarding their use—an area might have two dozen vans or small buses, owned by a dozen human service agencies and nonprofits, all running with just a few clients in each vehicle per trip.

U.S. Department of Transportation funding grants require a local match, usually 20 percent. That can be a problem in some areas. John Sorrell, transit manager for the Wiregrass Transit Authority in southeast Alabama, says, "It is extremely difficult for rural, agrarian, impoverished counties with low population density and a thin tax base to come up with a local match." In places with small annual budgets, he says, "that same match is also buying dump trucks, hiring deputy sheriffs, and paying for fire departments. If you go to voters and ask what they'd rather have, what do you think they'll say?"

Figure 2-4
This Chicago
Transit Authority
sign updates which
elevators are out
of order. Source:
Meghan Stromberg

SAFETEA-LU to the rescue?

Help may be available from SAFETEA-LU—Safe, Accountable, Flexible, Efficient Transportation Equity Act: A Legacy for Users. President Bush signed the law in 2005; funding goes through 2009. The law makes it easier for local transportation providers to share resources and loosens restrictions on the use of certain federal funds.

SAFETEA-LU requires that communities receiving Federal Transit Administration funds from the Elderly Individuals and Individuals with Disabilities program (section 5310), the Job Access and Reverse Commute Program (section 5316), or the New Freedom program (section 5317)—which was newly created under SAFETEA-LU—must create a locally developed Coordinated Human Services Transportation Plan. Receipt of FTA funding, starting with fiscal year 2007, is contingent on the submission of a coordinated plan.

A 2005 executive order also created the Interagency Transportation Coordinating Council on Access and Mobility, which, through a campaign called United We Ride, provides technical support and other information on coordination.

The goal of coordination planning, according to an FTA fact sheet, is to "enhance transportation access, minimize duplication of services, and facilitate the most appropriate cost-effective transportation possible with the available resources." That means transportation agencies, nonprofits, and human service providers must identify what service each is providing and to whom, and they must locate the gaps and redundancies. Citizens, business leaders, county agencies, county board members, and disability and senior advocacy groups must be involved in the process.

Finally, providers must work together to create a coordination plan that allows them to pool their resources—by sharing vehicles and funding, establishing a central dispatching mechanism, or any number of local innovations. "The coordinated plan is intended to identify areas where competing funding sources have stupid rules," says John Sorrell. "As it stands now, the elderly bus can't stop at a mental retardation facility to pick up riders, even though it's going the same way and there's only one person on the bus. SAFETEA-LU is committed to kicking those barriers to the curb."

Financing is flexible, too. Under the 2005 transportation reauthorization, communities may use federal funding from sources other than DOT, such as allocations from Medicaid, Medicare, and the Older Americans Act, to come up with a local match—generally 20 percent to the DOT's 80 percent. New Freedom program funds can also be used for operation costs in communities with populations under 200,000, rather than just capital expenses like buying new buses.

"Don't look at this process as SAFETEA-LU requiring these plans; look at it as an opportunity," says Roland Mross, a veteran federal and local transportation planner. Mross, who is now a United We Ride "ambassador," helping communities develop coordinated human service transportation plans, says that some places, particularly in Wisconsin and Washington, have taken the opportunity and run with it.

The Wisconsin Department of Transportation has taken the lead in helping the state's 72 counties create their coordination plans, with most plans being developed regionally in coordination with metropolitan planning organizations and regional planning commissions.

"We were the first in the nation to come out with a process," says Bobbie Beson-Crone, the manager of the Human Services Transportation Co-ordination program, a position recently created by WisDOT. The agency developed a toolkit for local planners to use and a set of worksheets to help various parties quantify and compare transportation services and costs. "This new process will give counties some data to use when they go to their boards asking for matching funds," Beson-Crone says.

No quick fix

Despite its benefits, coordination planning is no silver bullet. Unlike Wisconsin, most states have not made coordination planning a statewide priority. "One of the things that's been troublesome and a challenge for people at the local level is the question of who takes the lead," says Mross. "That can be a huge step to overcome."

In addition to technical support—such as United We Ride's "Framework for Action," a document many local governments use to formulate their plan—Mross says the campaign's ambassadors can deliver the occasional pep talk as new leaders emerge and communities work through the process.

Sometimes that encouragement is sorely needed. The executive summary of the Southeast Alabama Regional Planning and Development Commission's Human Services Transportation Coordination Plan paints a bleak picture: "Due to the lack of resources available locally, we found varying degrees of enthusiasm for the coordination process. For many, it was difficult to rationalize a coordination process when no resources or assets existed on the ground to be coordinated."

Among the barriers cited: the lack of funds to meet local match requirements, an increasingly larger and spread out rural elderly population, already over-extended senior transportation providers, and users' unrealistic expectations of extraordinary service.

Finally, there is the human dimension. Individuals are also important in creating a new transportation paradigm—one that relies less heavily on cars. "It is a personal responsibility," says AARP's Elinor Ginzler. "That's why we want our members to become active, to produce changes."

Meghan Stromberg is *Planning's* senior editor. This article was published in November 2007.

Volunteers make a difference

Volunteers play a big part in meeting local senior mobility needs. The Beverly Foundation, based in Pasadena, California, does a yearly survey of supplemental transportation programs for seniors, which includes information on volunteer driving programs. Its June 2006 survey of almost 500 drivers from 288 cities indicates that more than half are age 65 or older and that half volunteer at least one to five hours a week.

A case study in another 2006 report, "Transportation Innovations for Seniors: A Report from Rural America," published by the Beverly Foundation and the Community Transportation Association of America, highlighted a volunteer driver training program developed by the York County Community Action Corporation, in Sanford, Maine. The group's 90-plus volunteers must take four credit hours of driver training a year, in courses ranging from defensive driving and auto maintenance to CPR and dealing with the visually and hearing impaired.

In Eugene, Oregon, volunteers called Bus Buddies help seniors learn how to use public transportation—from planning the trip and reading bus schedules and maps to boarding and paying fares. They also explain the vehicles' accessibility features and how to get on and off the bus safely.

Another bus buddy program, this one in and around Appleton, Wisconsin, is part of a larger, privately funded initiative called Making the Ride Happen. It helps connect people age 60 and over with transportation options, including public transportation, senior buses, and a program called Senior Wheels, which relies exclusively on volunteer drivers using their own cars and gas.

Left Behind

The evacuation of New Orleans before Hurricane Katrina struck was both a great success and a miserable failure. Years of planning and coordination among transportation planners, emergency managers, and the police led to an effective contraflow system that gave anyone with a car the ability to evacuate. Unfortunately, the carless were literally left behind.

In the days following the hurricane, the world watched in disbelief as all systems indiscriminately failed to respond, affecting young, elderly, poor, tourists, and the disabled alike. However, seniors living independently were disproportionately victims of the flood. As I evacuated, I recall feeling guilty and somewhat responsible that my profession, transportation planning, failed to deliver an effective plan for a disaster that everyone knew would happen. It became part of my mission to ensure that we do not repeat past mistakes—not just in New Orleans but across the country.

Within days of the storm I launched the Transportation Equity and Evacuation Planning Program at the University of New

Orleans Transportation Center. Its charge is to provide research and outreach to improve evacuation planning and practice for all members of society. In the research I have conducted since Katrina, I have come to learn that New Orleans is not unique when it comes to its carless population or disaster vulnerability. Cities like New York and Washington, D.C., have no option but to learn from our lessons. And as our population ages, the risks are even greater.

In February 2007, the UNOTC hosted the first National Conference on Disaster Planning for the Carless Society, which brought together planners, emergency managers, and transportation and health care providers. Speakers and attendees at this conference represented a diverse group of stakeholders from nonprofit organizations, government, universities, and the community. Not surprisingly, a variety of topics surrounding carless evacuation were widely discussed. (A free webcast of all presentations can be downloaded at www.carlessevacuation.org/Program.htm.)

The UNOTC is also leading a four-year national study of carless evacuation planning, sponsored by a grant from the Federal Transit Administration. Our goal, in both the conference and research, is to bridge the transportation, emergency management, and health care professions as well as establish communication among local, parish/county, state, and federal governments. The FTA grant will focus on carless evacuation efforts in Chicago, Miami, New Orleans, New York, and San Francisco.

On August 16, 2007, we conducted the first set of focus groups in New Orleans. One meeting brought together leaders from the nonprofit community and the other involved government representatives. The nonprofit meeting revealed an interesting dynamic in post-Katrina New Orleans: Although confidence was high regarding recent government efforts to create a carless and special needs evacuation plan, most community agencies said they would not rely on the government in the event of a hurricane because they have created their own plans. Virtually all community nonprofits noted that while they feel prepared for hurricane evacuation, which allows for a warning period, no-notice emergencies would present a serious challenge.

The government focus group (which included a representative from the private motor coach industry) exposed a continual disconnect between federal, state, and local policy. While officials from all levels of government called for better federal guidance on these issues, one of the most important issues in planning for carless evacuation remains a local issue: the identification of carless people who need help.

This fall, our team will be conducting focus groups and interviews in all five cities. The Center for Hazards Assessment, Response and Technology at UNO is working closely with the university's transportation center. CHART is focusing on a number of local and regional carless evacuation planning issues, including issues surrounding elderly evacuation.

For more information on the FTA carless evacuation study, contact John Renne at jrenne@uno.edu.

John Renne, AICP

John Renne is assistant professor of Urban Planning and Transportation Studies and associate director of the University of New Orleans Transportation Center. He wrote a diary of the days before and after Hurricane Katrina; "Evacuation and Equity" ran in the May 2006 issue of *Planning*.

Resources

National organizations. AARP's research on senior transportation is at www.aarp.org/research/housing-mobility/transportation/. The Beverly Foundation is at www.beverlyfoundation.org. Community Transportation Association of America: www.ctaa. org. MIT's AgeLab: http://web.mit.edu/agelab/.

State and region. Wisconsin's coordination planning toolkit and other resources are online at www.dot.state.wi.us/localgov/transit/specialized.htm. Northern Virginia Transportation Commission senior mobility report: www.thinkoutsidethecar.org/research/completed_research.asp.

More. The Surface Transportation Policy Partnership's "Stranded Without Options" report is at www.transact.org/report.asp?id=232.

DISPLACED AND REPLACED

Where are all those public housing residents now?

By James Krohe Jr.

HOPE VI (Housing Opportunities for People Everywhere) was conceived in 1992 as the final fix for failed public housing in America. Under the program of federal grants, "highly distressed" public housing projects are leveled and replaced by new mixed income communities. The federal government has so far spent well over $5 billion on HOPE VI housing, and various studies confirm that the program has benefited dozens of cities: The new housing has meant less crime and more economic activity in surrounding neighborhoods.

But what about the people who lived in the old housing projects? Where do they go while their former homes are being razed and rebuilt? Are residents—many of whom spent their whole lives in public housing—equipped to find or keep housing outside the projects? And if they want to go back home, will there be a home for them?

Everyone needs a home

"Everyone displaced from a HOPE VI site must have housing," says Rosalind Braithwaite, relocation coordinator for the District of Columbia Housing Authority. "We can offer them a choice of other public housing," she says, "or a voucher and assistance in finding housing in the private sector." After the rebuilding phase, former residents can—if there are units available and they meet the eligibility requirements—leave those temporary lodgings and move back into their now-spiffed-up former homes.

The U.S. Department of Housing and Urban Development, HOPE VI's parent, does not track the fates of former residents nationally, and thus does not know exactly which of these choices displaced residents opt for. In 2001, the first systematic, multicity study of HOPE VI's impact on original residents was undertaken by the Urban Institute. The institute tracked more than 800 former residents of five mostly modest-sized HOPE VI projects in five states to see how residents had fared since their projects were transformed.

"We're the only one who has data," says Susan Popkin, an Urban Institute senior research associate. Researchers found that of the 818 households interviewed, 19 percent were living in redeveloped HOPE VI projects, 29 percent in other public housing, 33 percent were living in private market housing, and 18 percent had left assisted housing.

That information is now several years old, however. Today, many sites are still being redeveloped, and the relocation services offered to displaced households have, generally, been improved. Resettlement patterns also vary from city to city depending on the local housing market, the quality of available housing stock, and the effectiveness of the counseling and relocation services provided by the public housing authority. Still, the Urban Institute findings are confirmed in broad terms by local tracking studies and other data.

'Opportunity communities'

One of the ambitions of the HOPE VI program is to give residents better lives in neighborhoods that are less segregated, less poor, and better served by social services than the old projects. The means of escape to these "opportunity communities" is the "housing choice," or Section 8, voucher (which provides a federal rent subsidy).

Confirming the Urban Institute figures, the National Housing Law Project found in 2002 that about 30 percent of displaced residents had relocated to privately owned rental units with the help of Section 8 vouchers.

"A lot of former residents prefer the voucher program," says Popkin. "As our data show, they end up in much better quality housing." Better, at least, than the old projects from which they came. Former tenants often wind up in larger quarters than they had in public housing. Just as important, they usually are located in safer neighborhoods.

Columbia University sociologists Sudhir Venkatesh and Isil Celimli have been tracking tenants displaced by Chicago's HOPE VI program from the condemned Robert Taylor Homes on the South Side. Venkatesh reports that about 20 to 25 percent claim dramatic improvements in their living situation.

"This is not insignificant," Venkatesh has said, but "it certainly is not stellar." In the early years of the program, most former tenants in Chicago opting for Section 8 vouchers ended up in neighborhoods that, while not as grim as the worst public housing projects, were still poor and still mostly minority.

That was true in many cities. Popkin notes that the new housing of her sample population, while safer, was far from safe (40 percent reported serious problems with gangs and drug trafficking).

Why do so many displaced families end up in neighborhoods that frustrate the larger social aims of the HOPE VI program? There are lots of reasons: inadequate relocation services, too-rapid move-out timetables (which leave tenants with too little time to find alternatives), and cozy relationships between relocation counselors and certain landlords. Also, many landlords are reluctant to rent to public housing tenants or families with many children.

"To a large extent, the success of HOPE VI depends on the availability of replacement housing," says Popkin. But there aren't many Section 8 properties available in better neighborhoods. As has been pointed out by the contributors to *Where Are Poor People To Live?*, a new book about the Chicago experience, many of the new housing units being built in cities lately are for high-end renters and owners. A common result is that HOPE VI families with vouchers end up in neighborhoods with willing landlords—and that usually means neighborhoods only slightly better than the projects they left.

In addition, discrimination real or perceived still limits housing choice. Poor and African American households are much less likely to move into "opportunity communities" than are families of other races. Welfare families of any color also have tended to avoid more affluent neighborhoods.

This finding is widely attributed to lack of social support before and after the move. However, there is evidence that public housing residents do what most people do—seek out neighborhoods with people pretty much like themselves. As Meghan Harte, CHA's director of resident services, has explained, many public housing families don't see their communities as isolated, poor, and segregated.

When the Housing Authority of Portland, Oregon, began to HOPE VI its 462-unit Columbia Villa project on the city's north side, 93 percent of the residents expressed a preference to relocate to North Portland, whether with Section 8 vouchers or by transferring to other HAP properties in the area. The reasons? To keep the kids in the same schools, be near family, and avoid discrimination.

Back to the projects

All HOPE VI projects have some redeveloped public housing units to which former residents can return. Some public housing authorities guarantee displaced residents a spot if they want to return, while some merely place them at the top of the waiting lists for new housing in the reborn projects.

A few public housing authorities have been able to replace razed units one for one. One factor is the commitment of local government. In Boston, explains Boston Housing Authority spokesperson Lydia Agro, "It was a policy decision to bring back as many [units] as possible. The housing authority and the mayor are committed to preserving affordable housing for people who need it"—especially, she says, because there is "a serious affordable housing crisis in Boston."

In Washington, says District of Columbia Housing Authority executive director Michael Kelly, AICP, "for families whose income is zero to 30 percent of the median, we're the only game in town."

Another factor behind one-for-one replacement is the vigor of the local residential real estate market. In Washington, the returns from market rate rents in the mixed income communities that replace the old projects and the ability to capitalize on valuable land have allowed public housing authorities to replace most or all of the original units, despite the cost. At the Arthur Capper and Carrollsburg Dwellings, a 23-acre public housing complex in Near Southeast, a $34.9 million HOPE VI grant has been leveraged into a total expenditure of $424 million; 758 demolished units will be replaced with 707 public housing units (plus 525 affordable rental units and 330 market rate houses), making it the first HOPE VI site in the nation to provide nearly one-for-one replacement of demolished public housing units.

Figure 2-5
The future community marketplace (with apartments above). Source: Mike Wert, Housing Authority of Portland

Adrianne Todman, deputy chief of staff at DCHA, explains the secret behind housing lots of poor families without creating new ghettoes: "Land, land, land and density, density, density is the magic answer," she says.

At the Arthur Capper and Carrollsburg Dwellings, she notes, the original footprint was expanded to accommodate 1,600 new units on site. "The new units look like [town houses on] Capitol Hill but might be housing two families," she adds.

"We're committed to a providing a mix of one-third low-income, a third moderate-income, and a third market rate units," says Kelly, "which we can do by expanding the scale."

In cities where local rents are so high or Section 8 landlords so scarce that public housing residents have few private-market alternatives (as in the San Francisco Bay Area), a fair number do go back—if their housing authority provides plenty of units for households eligible for public housing.

You can't go home again

By the time rebuilding is done at most HOPE VI sites, however, few former public housing residents end up back at those sites—only 19 percent by 2001, according to the Urban Institute. The National Housing Law Project survey found only 11.4 percent of former residents overall have returned or are expected to return to HOPE VI sites.

Why so few? For one thing, many of the residents who want to move back after reconstruction aren't in assisted housing programs by the time the new units are ready. In some cities the attrition rate—households that cease to be eligible for public-housing—approaches 50 percent over the course of a HOPE VI redevelopment.

Some of the "lost" displaced are people who have broken their lease in some way, or who left public housing for private housing. Other Section 8 users find they prefer not having to deal with public housing bureaucracies and rules.

Where alternative housing is available and acceptable, still others find it too difficult to move back. Some get discouraged by long delays in reconstruction. (The wait between relocation and reoccupancy in some cities has been as long as six years.)

Local housing authorities that were unable to manage the day-to-day operations of conventional public housing complexes often have proved no better at managing relocation and resettlement of dozens, even hundreds, of families. In several well-publicized cases, former residents couldn't be notified that new units were available because the authority lost track of them. This matters, because only those families who remain connected to the housing authority will be notified of social services, relocation assistance, and the availability of a new place to live in the old neighborhood.

Among the households that do wish to move back, many cannot find a place, since far fewer public housing units are built in most HOPE VI projects than are torn down. And even when a new unit is available, it may not fit their needs, or they cannot meet the stricter eligibility requirements that their public housing authority insists on.

Atlanta's ambitious HOPE VI program is fairly typical. About 6,400 public housing rental units will be replaced with some 5,800 mixed income rental units, only 2,300 of which will be reserved for public-housing-eligible households.

Figure 2-6
New Columbia, a HOPE VI project in Portland, Oregon, includes 556 affordable rentals and 232 for-sale homes. In the park is a sculpture by Nanda D'Agostino. Source: Mike Wert, Housing Authority of Portland

In addition, HOPE VI sites are sometimes rebuilt using relatively small, land-efficient town houses—inappropriate for large families. (Return rates have been higher when residents have been consulted about design; in some cities, residents have argued for town houses that can be connected to accommodate large families.)

"How many return?" asks the AHA's Rick White rhetorically. "One hundred percent of those who are eligible and want to. That's very few." The key word here is "eligible." "To qualify for the new housing," Susan Popkin explains, "authorities impose pretty strict standards."

Eligibility hurdles

Reoccupancy eligibility standards vary from city to city. In Raleigh, North Carolina, where the Raleigh Housing Authority is rebuilding the 296-unit Chavis Heights public housing complex, applicants for units in the new and improved version who are under the age of 65 must be employed.

The Chicago Housing Authority standards are especially stringent. All renters interested in living in its new mixed income communities, including CHA families, must have a head of household who is at least 18 years old and works at least 30 hours a week, be current in rent and utility bills (a big problem because surveys show that a third of public housing residents in Chicago had unpaid utility bills), have no bankruptcies within the past two years, and owe no debt to any public housing program. CHA families are assisted by a team of service providers and counselors to meet these requirements.

Perhaps the biggest single factor in keeping displaced residents from moving back to HOPE VI sites is tenant screening requirements. Larry Keating, FAICP, an emeritus professor in the City and Regional Planning Program at the Georgia Institute of Technology, is a vocal critic of Atlanta's HOPE VI program. He blames what he calls "intensified lease provision enforcement" for the fact that so few original residents make it back to redeveloped sites.

Rick White of the Atlanta Housing Authority finds that criticism "almost ridiculous." He adds: "We insist that tenants can't be engaged in ongoing criminal activity, and we do require adults 18 to 62 have a job or be in job training or school that leads to an outcome."

White says that the rate of return is a false indicator of success or failure of a HOPE VI project in any event. "The premise is dubious," he says. "It assumes that families belong in government housing. We don't assume that."

What is success?

Such numbers—fewer units, few returnees—are proof of a failed program, in the opinion of HOPE VI's many critics. But in terms of the program's original premise, those numbers suggest success. One of the purposes of the authorizing act, after all, was to deconcentrate poverty in such sites.

Section 24 of the Quality Housing and Work Responsibility Act of 1998 lists among the purposes of HOPE VI to be "providing housing that will avoid or decrease the concentration of very low-income families" and thus to break up the often toxic concentrations of the very poor and attendant drug use and crime that made the projects a misery for the people who lived in them. "The idea of putting the same number of low-income folks back in redeveloped sites made no sense," says Mike Kelly of the District of Columbia Housing Authority.

Larry Keating chaired the Atlanta Gentrification Task Force, a city-appointed committee, from 2000 to 2001. His work on the force prompted him to complain that HOPE VI often destroyed indigenous communities that, while poor, still functioned socially. "Destruction of social communities is something that we supposedly decided not to do any more after the disastrous experiences with urban renewal," he says now.

Keating is not alone in that criticism. A 2004 lawsuit filed by the Legal Assistance Foundation of Chicago on behalf of CHA tenants alleged that families asked to leave the notorious Cabrini-Green project, by being removed from support networks of family and friends, were at risk of becoming more transient and more detached from the world of work, school, and social services—even homeless.

Figure 2-7
Some New Columbia residents at play. Source: Mike Wert, Housing Authority of Portland

The hard-to-house

"The ones that are left are the hard-to-house population, and most end up in public housing again," says Popkin. A report by the General Accounting Office, using HUD data, stated that most of the 49,000 residents that had been relocated from HOPE VI sites had ended up in other traditional public housing by June 2003. The percentage varies from project to project and city to city.

Who are the hard-to-house? They tend to be people with histories of joblessness, drug use, or gang involvement, who have been evicted from housing authority property, people who lack the social skills and education to cope with life in private housing, and those who cannot come close to qualifying for places in HOPE VI mixed income projects.

Health is also a problem. Popkin notes rates of obesity, hypertension, diabetes, and depression that are significantly higher even than the already high levels found among poor and minority groups in general. Also in the hard-to-house category are grandparents caring for grandchildren, families with disabled members, and very large households. Many of them are, in the words of the Urban Institute study, "literally one step away from becoming homeless."

Popkin and colleagues found that Chicago has particularly large proportions of hard-to-house families, but they also found that to be true of at least 40 percent of the residents at all five studied sites. "The problem of hard-to-house residents in HOPE VI sites is widespread," they concluded, "and the need for alternative relocation options is significant."

"It is safe to say that nobody could have truly understood how devastating the effects have been of economic and social isolation on generations of families," says Rick White of Atlanta. "We expected that making sure they had access to great schools, job training, child care, and so on would be enough. We didn't realize that there are still barriers beyond that."

All agree that equipping such families to take advantage of the opportunities that a well-run HOPE VI program offers will take intensive (and expensive) social services, larger units in HOPE VI developments, and both transitional and permanent "supportive" housing. "You have to have grants," says Kelly. "The ongoing operations cost of housing the very low [income] tier is very expensive."

The problem is that HOPE VI has been targeted for elimination by the Bush administration, and while Congress has continued to authorize it anyway, the program has been funded at ever-lower levels for years. It would be a cruel twist if HOPE VI, by making the worst of the nation's failed public housing projects better places to live, would end up making the rest of them worse by turning them into dumping grounds for ever denser concentrations of the hard-to-house.

James Krohe Jr. is a Chicago-based freelance writer. This article was published in December 2006.

A Daunting Task

Relocating tens of thousands of public housing residents during HOPE VI rebuilding was always going to be a daunting task. Consider Chicago's Plan of Transformation (the nation's biggest HOPE VI program). Alex Kotlowitz, who has written extensively about public housing residents, notes that the Chicago Housing Authority housed 200,000 people when HOPE VI was passed: "It's the equivalent of tearing down a city with the population of Des Moines."

The Chicago Housing Authority delegates management of its "Housing Opportunity" voucher program to the private contractor CHAC Inc., which runs one of the largest mobility-counseling programs in the country, serving some 10,000 voucher holders.

In Boston, demolition of the 413-unit Maverick Gardens public housing project required that residents relocate either temporarily or permanently to other housing. Lydia Agro of the Boston Housing Authority says relocation tasks were handled by Housing Opportunities Unlimited, a Boston-based firm that has helped move more HOPE VI residents than any other company in the U.S. "They're experts, they're bilingual, they want to do what's right for every household," she says.

HOU provided five full-time staff people on-site, counseled residents during the reoccupancy process, conducted housekeeping and budgeting workshops with follow-up counseling, and assisted with school transfer requests, utility hook-ups, and fee reduction requests.

While former Chicago Housing Authority tenants with Section 8 vouchers are soaking up all the available low-rent housing in certain parts of the city, poor families without subsidies are forced to look for housing out of town. Some are moving to downstate Illinois cities such as Danville, Rantoul, Champaign-Urbana, and Bloomington-Normal, some 140 miles away. The result, local officials report, is an increase in the number of special needs kids in local schools, more criminals with links to Chicago, demand for public housing and Section 8 vouchers that often exceeds supplies, and a burden on budgets of local social service agencies.

Resources
Online. Atlanta Public Housing Authority: www.atlantahousingauth.org. Boston Housing Authority: www.bostonhousing.org. Chicago Public Housing Authority: www.cha.org. District of Columbia Housing Authority: www.dchousing.org. Housing Authority of Portland (Oregon): www.hapdx.org. National Housing Law Project (based in Oakland, California): www.nhlp.org. Urban Institute (based in Washington, D.C.): www.urban.org.
Reading. *Where Are Poor People to Live?*, published last spring, was edited by Larry Bennett, Janet Smith, and Patricia Wright. Alexander Polikoff's recent book, *Waiting for Gautreaux,* describes the battle over segregated public housing in Chicago. Alex Kotlowitz's 1992 book, *There Are No Children Here,* describes life in Chicago's Henry Horner Homes.

LOCKED UP, THEN LOCKED OUT

Experts say residency restrictions for sex offenders may create more problems than they solve.

By Meghan Stromberg

James Hill was set to be released from prison in the summer of 2005 and had arranged for post-incarceration housing at a mission. But on the day of his release, Hill (not his real name) learned from prison authorities that he wasn't allowed to live at the shelter. His choice was either to find appropriate housing or be transferred to another prison until he could. "I'd already been in prison for 16 years; I didn't want to stay any longer," he said in a phone interview.

That's when Hill's struggle to find a place to live began. His family's house was within 1,000 feet of a school, and a state law—passed after his conviction—prohibited Hill, a sex offender, from living there. He moved temporarily into an overpriced trailer in the middle of nowhere, he says, but his family eventually moved so that he could live with them. Shortly after moving in, his parole officer told him the new house was off-limits because it was less than 1,000 feet from a playground. "But I knew enough about the planning office and GIS to ask a planner there to give me a reading," Hill says. It was 1,323 feet away, and he was allowed to stay.

Hill's contact with the planning office was resourceful but not random after he received an undergraduate degree then worked with GIS, helping to digitize county maps.

Hill says he's fortunate to have a supportive family. Even so, he says that laws that restrict where he can—and more precisely, cannot—live are unfair and ineffective. "Everywhere you turn there's a school or a park [going up.] It's a felony for me to live [near one]," he says.

But is a convicted sex offender's challenge in finding housing a planning problem? "It's most definitely a planning issue," Hill adds. "What if I'd owned property before I went to prison?" Besides, he says, "my crime had nothing to do with where I live. Putting those restrictions on people like me doesn't help keep the community safer—in fact, they give people a false sense of security."

Hill was convicted of molesting a child in his family. Like him, the vast majority of sex offenders aren't strangers—experts say that 90 percent of them know their victims or are related to them.

"I'm not asking anyone to feel sorry for me. I did the crime and I'm paying the price, but I think [the government] crossed the line."

Yes, in your backyard

It's difficult to feel sympathy for people like Hill, who have hurt children or sexually assaulted adults. Highly publicized cases like that of Jessica Lunsford, a Florida girl who in 2005 was abducted, assaulted, and buried alive by a convicted sex offender, keep violent sex crimes in the news.

While sexual abuse has dropped 40 percent in the last two decades, according to the U.S. Department of Justice, few jurisdictions are prepared when convicted sex offenders are released from prison and reenter the community.

Twenty-one states and hundreds of municipalities have passed laws restricting where sex offenders can live. Do they work? Do they make communities safer? Many places think so and are passing residency laws at a steady clip, in many cases competing to craft more restrictive laws than the next town over.

Still, residency restrictions have their critics. Making sections of a city uninhabitable to sex offenders greatly reduces offenders' access to housing, employment, transportation, and services. Those who treat sex offenders say that situation creates more problems: Without support, stable housing, jobs, and access to treatment, sex offenders—and all criminals—are statistically more likely to commit new crimes. They are also more likely to go underground, making it impossible to monitor them.

Released sex offenders live in every state. "We want to believe they are the few, the perverted, and the far away," says David D'Amora, a therapist who works with sex offenders in Connecticut and chairs the public policy committee of the Association for the Treatment of Sexual Abusers, based in Beaverton, Oregon. In fact, there are more than half a million registered sex offenders nationwide, with more than 100,000 in California alone.

How the laws have evolved

Since 1994, sex offenders have been required to register with local authorities on a regular basis. The federal law passed that year, the Jacob Wetterling Crimes Against Children and Sexually Violent Offender Registration Act, is named after an 11-year-old Minnesota boy who was abducted and never found. While U.S. law compels sex offenders to register, state laws dictate how often and for how long; 11 states require lifetime registration.

A 1996 amendment to the Jacob Wetterling Act, Megan's Law, added a community notification requirement, which also varies by state. Most states publish an online database of sex offenders' names, addresses, and convictions, whereas others leave it to local authorities to circulate information to nearby neighbors or schools. The law is named after the high-profile case of Megan Kanka, a seven-year-old New Jersey girl who was raped and killed by a known sex offender who had moved in across the street from her family.

With Megan's Law, "we created an opportunity for the public to know where sex offenders live," says Suzanne Brown-McBride, a victims advocate and executive director of CALCASA, the California Coalition Against Sexual Assault. She notes that no other class of criminals, including murderers, is similarly monitored.

But, says Brown-McBride, the registry stirs up all sorts of NIMBY issues, with opponents of this unwanted population mounting fierce, highly emotional arguments. "As a consequence of these laws, no one wants to live by them," she says. "That's where it becomes a planning problem. From the outset, you've got competing goals"—tracking where offenders live in the community, but also letting community members know where they are.

Child safety zones and residency restrictions emerged in 2000, Brown-McBride says. "They followed the model of nuisance codes, places with drug-free and prostitute-free zones. Some states did it very narrowly—around schools and day care centers. Others made it almost impossible to live anywhere."

Today's residency laws assume that reducing the likelihood of contact with children will reduce the chance of abuse. These "distance marker" laws typically prohibit known sex offenders from living—and sometimes working or loitering—within a certain distance of schools, day care centers, and "places where children congregate." They may also specifically include parks, certain public areas, churches, and school bus stops. The least restrictive distance marker ordinances mandate a 500-foot buffer, but distances of 1,000 and 2,500 feet are common.

Several of the laws have withstood constitutional challenges. The most notable is in Iowa, where registered sex offenders are prohibited from living within 2,000 feet of a school, day care provider, or park. In 2005, the Eighth Circuit Court of Appeals upheld the state law as constitutional in *Doe v. Miller*, after a suit was brought by the ACLU. The court concluded that the law did not amount to "punishment" and declared that the Constitution does not guarantee a "right to live where you choose."

Critics have charged that residency laws amount to banishment. Courts have disagreed. Proponents of the laws argue that "if you draw circles around schools, there still may be pockets where sex offenders can live," says Stephen JohnsonGrove, an attorney with the Ohio Justice and Policy Center. He notes that the laws are made possible by technology used by planners every day. "These laws exist only because GIS exists. There's no way they'd send a surveyor to evaluate every sex offender's living situation. But with GIS, it's easy to do."

Figure 2-8
Sex offenders are put on notice outside a park in Franklin Township, New Jersey.
Source: Dith Pram, The New York Times

JohnsonGrove is working with sex offenders challenging Ohio's residency law, which went into effect in 2005. That state, as well as Kentucky, Georgia, and Oklahoma, has no provision for grandfathering in sex offenders who lived within a buffer zone when the law was passed. One client is 75 and has lived in his house for 35 years. He says that offenders in those situations "come to us because they are being thrown out. We're not challenging whether they committed an offense or not, but [this] violates the ex post facto clause—you can't impose punishment after the fact."

Broad brush

Some states and cities have opted not to pass residency laws. Covington, Kentucky, a Cincinnati suburb, defeated such an ordinance in spring 2005. The proposed law would have created a 2,000-foot buffer (Kentucky's law is 1,000 feet). Alex Edmondson, a city commissioner, was an opponent, he says, because it would have forced people to move. By drawing up maps of the city and overlaying school buffer zones, the city also found that most local sex offenders would be concentrated in one residential area.

Colorado and Minnesota chose not to enact residency laws after commissioning studies of the regulations' effectiveness. In Colorado, research showed that second-time offenders did not live any closer to a school than those who did not reoffend. Both states' studies noted that residency restrictions tended to isolate offenders, driving them into rural places, or areas lacking jobs, transportation, and treatment providers. They found that the laws significantly reduced offenders' access to affordable housing.

Sex offender residency laws sound good in theory, says Jill Levenson, a researcher at Lynn University in Boca Raton, Florida, who is considered an expert on the topic. "They grow out of fear, out of anger at an abhorrent criminal—often a [person who has hurt] a child. The media perpetuates this perception that all offenders reoffend, that treatment doesn't help, and that [these people have] fixed and unchangeable characteristics."

She goes on to say that there is no doubt that some sex offenders are highly dangerous and likely to commit more crimes, but notes that sex offenders are actually a heterogeneous group. "Residency laws tend to be overly inclusive. When we lump [all sex offenders] together, it dilutes the ability of the public to tell who is truly a risk," she says. Laws should target supervision and management pertinent to an individual's offense pattern, she adds.

What is the recidivism rate among sex offenders? A 2004 study by Andrew Harris and Karl Hanson of Public Safety and Emergency Preparedness Canada, a government agency, notes that the question is not easily answered because the offenders—their age, sex, previous criminal history, relationship to the victims—vary greatly. The age and sex of victims and the types of crimes are also factors.

Using data from 10 follow-up studies of adult male offenders, Harris and Hanson's study found that most did not commit new sex crimes. First-time offenders are less likely to reoffend than those with previous sexual convictions and younger offenders are more likely to commit new offenses.

The likelihood of recidivism decreases the longer a convicted offender lives in the community. Fifteen years following an offender's release, 13 percent of incestuous child molesters commit new sex crimes (six percent of them in the first five years). Among molesters with girl victims, 16 percent reoffend within 15 years. Among those with boy victims, that figure is 35 percent (23 percent in the first five years).

'Stranger danger'

The most glaring mismatch between broad distance marker laws that prohibit sex offenders from being near schools is the fact that very few children are actually snatched from schools—or anywhere else—and assaulted by strangers. According to the U.S. Bureau of Justice, just over 90 percent of all sex crimes against children are committed by a family member or an acquaintance. (In cases of assault against adults, that number is lower—70 to 75 percent.)

"It's the stranger offenses that seem to be the motivation for the legislation, yet the majority of offenses are perpetrated by offenders known to the victim," says Charles Onley, a research associate at the Center for Sex Offender Management, a project supported by the Office of Justice Programs at the Department of Justice. "The research is there. A lot of the residency restrictions are impacting people who perpetrated these acts because they had access; they were in a position of trust and had fostered a relationship," he adds.

David D'Amora also notes that national studies estimate that 85 percent of victims never report the crime. "A female or child is at a greater risk of being attacked by a never-arrested person than a convicted sex offender," he says.

Of course, not all sex crimes involve children; 33 percent of victims of any type of sexual assault are over 18, according to the Bureau of Justice National Incidence-Based Reporting System. Yet, buffer laws do not protect places where potential adult victims congregate, nor do most differentiate between sex offenders who offend against children and those who assault adults.

Unintended consequences

Residency restrictions can do more harm than good, say some sexual abuse experts. "There are a number of unintended consequences to offenders that the public and politicians aren't all that sympathetic to," says Jill Levenson. Chief among them, as the Colorado and Minnesota studies note, is offenders' limited access to affordable housing, and sometimes, housing of any kind.

Depending how a city is laid out, a distance marker law can virtually exclude sex offenders. Proposition 83, a bill passed overwhelmingly by California voters in November, increases the state's distance marker law, now prohibiting residences within 2,000 feet of a school. It also mandates longer sentences and requires all sex offenders to be monitored with GPS. The law makes most of Los Angeles, San Francisco, and San Diego, as well as the central areas of other cities, off-limits to sex offenders.

The consequences of being zoned out of affordable housing are three-fold, experts say. Registered sex offenders unable to find housing in the cities and suburbs are pushed into rural areas, where access to transportation and jobs may be scarce. Counselors and other treatment providers, as well as a reliable support group of peers and family, might also be out of reach. Yet, stable housing, employment, support, and treatment are all proven positive factors in the rehabilitation of offenders, Levenson says.

The law also puts offenders at risk of becoming homeless. In October, an informal review of the Iowa Sex Offender Registry for Polk County, where Des Moines is located, showed that five of the 473 registered offenders listed their address as "homeless." Others claimed a motley assortment of living arrangements: 25 lived in motels, four at rest areas, and five in trucks, cars, or tents. Two offenders listed their address as "under Interstate bridge off northeast 14th Street."

Offenders are also slipping off the law enforcement community's radar, making monitoring impossible. On Polk County's website, more than 35 offenders' addresses simply read "whereabouts unknown," a registry category that is growing rapidly in Iowa.

Last January, the Iowa County Attorneys Association released a public statement denouncing the 2,000-foot ban. In addition to the objections mentioned above, it adds that law enforcement budgets are being strained by the laws without providing any "demonstrated protective effect." The statement also notes that the laws punish families of offenders, "whose lives are unfairly and unnecessarily disrupted by the restriction, causing children to be pulled out of school and away from friends, and causing spouses to lose jobs and community connections."

What's a city to do?

The political pressure to keep sex offenders away is intense, as Alex Edmondson, the Covington, Kentucky, commissioner who came out against a local law, can attest.

In September, O'Fallon, Missouri, passed a law that surpasses the state law, creating a 2,000-foot buffer around day care centers and a 3,000-foot zone around schools, libraries, pools, and parks. Earlier that month in the *St. Louis Post-Dispatch*, city council member Pierce Conley summed up the commonly held view among many politicians and citizens: "I just don't see why anyone would vote against it. It's kind of like speaking against the flag, for God's sake."

Now cities are competing to make ever stricter regulations ensuring that sex offenders stay out of *their* town. Within less than a month of the approval of the O'Fallon law, another Charles County city, Dardenne Prairie, followed suit. Four other municipalities either have bills in the works or are considering drafting proposals, according to the *Post-Dispatch*.

"From a victim's advocate point of view, it is not acceptable for one community to push out offenders and say, 'We're going to protect our kids but not yours,'" says CALCASA's Suzanne Brown-McBride.

"What residency restrictions tend to do is make people pretend there's nowhere," she adds. "What planning forces you to do is find somewhere." Both Brown-McBride and her colleague, CALCASA director of public affairs Robert Coombs, say planners are an untapped resource in the struggle to find housing situations that are suitable for offenders and acceptable to the community. "Planners are masterful at those conversations," says Coombs. "They understand community dynamics and the difficulty of putting in something that people don't want." Planners may also appreciate how good placement can actually enhance community safety.

Figure 2-9
On one residential street in Davenport, Iowa, a dozen sex offenders live in apartment buildings like this one. Detective Rich Tubbs says released offenders call the police looking for legal housing. Source: Meghan Stromberg

Brown-McBride advises thinking ahead, noting that it is easy to find information on the number of local sex offenders in prison and the length of their sentences. Group homes or other facilities can be planned, zoning can be changed to allow more flexible land uses, and community education can begin—long before a sex offender's imminent return sparks a crisis. She notes that planning and law enforcement can build stronger connections, perhaps by locating police substations in areas where housing for sex offenders is also planned.

"In places where proactive planning has not happened, sex offenders and unwanted populations of all kinds tend to go into places that are low-income, fragile, stressed," Brown-McBride says. She notes that some local planning efforts—such as a facility for sexually violent predators—are under way, but few broad initiatives exist.

Brown-McBride goes so far as to suggest that zoning might be relaxed to allow sex offenders to live in a light industrial area rather than a residential zone. James Hill, the convicted sex offender familiar with GIS and planning issues, takes issue with that. "A light industrial area? That makes me not a person, but a thing. Does that make it easier for people? I find that appalling."

On the other hand, "is it better than not having a place at all? Well yes, of course it is," he admits.

As a sex offender treatment provider, David D'Amora frequently works with victims' advocates, police and parole officers, and local governments to conduct community education sessions, both before a crisis happens and in the midst of one. He suggests a different approach. "Defining this as a criminal justice problem is a terrible mistake. This should be a public health issue," he says.

"The problem with residency restrictions is that they almost always accomplish the opposite" of what they are intended to do, he adds. "Interventions like these actually increase risk. If we truly care about public safety, we need to understand that we've put policies in place that make communities less safe."

Meghan Stromberg is *Planning's* senior editor. This article was published in January 2007.

Group Homes Still Struggle to Fit In

The family that lives at 61st Street and San Pablo Avenue in Oakland, California, is unusually large. Its household members occupy some 21 beds in a two-story Victorian house across from a school. The family is disciplined—breakfast is at 7:30 sharp, lunch at 1:30—and it's also friendly, with someone almost always on the front stoop to greet passersby.

But under many city codes this household would not qualify as a family. After all, its members are not related by blood, but rather by a common goal: to overcome the obstacles created by mental illness and substance abuse so that they can function in society.

The house is a group home called Morning Star Villa. Group homes, ranging from a few beds to a couple dozen, house those who, because of an addiction or a disability, can't otherwise live independently. Over the past few decades, more and more disabled people have left institutions and moved into small group living situations.

Like most group homes, Morning Star Villa does share aspects of a family, including mutual support, many long-term residents, and life skills education—"stuff to get them familiar with society," says administrator Anthony Piano. But group homes are a different animal: Drug dealers target them. Most residents need caseworkers. And the homes have unique real estate needs such as large buildings and inexpensive property.

That's the dilemma for planners used to cut-and-dried land-use categories. The 1988 federal Fair Housing Amendments Act classified people with disabilities as a protected class for which cities must make "a reasonable accommodation" in their zoning codes. A 1995 U.S. Supreme Court case upheld the FHAA's application to zoning. But nearly two decades after the FHAA became law, local governments are still struggling with how to regulate group homes.

"A lot more cities are allowing community residences as residential uses, but many are getting it wrong," says Daniel Lauber, AICP, a planner and attorney who specializes in community residence regulation. "The FHAA left people very confused."

Community integration

Group homes are part of a larger category known as community residences, which also includes halfway houses, a more temporary type of group living situation. Community residences have existed in the U.S. since the 1880s, says Lauber, but until the 1960s most policies leaned toward institutionalization for people with disabilities. In the 1960s and 70s that changed, as parents of people with disabilities filed lawsuits seeking alternatives to institutions.

"The key to all of this is community integration," Lauber says, helping to "make people all they can be." However, local governments lagged in regulating the growing number of community residences.

"Group homes were an anathema," says Martin Jaffe, an associate professor of urban planning and policy at the University of Illinois–Chicago. Generally, he says, group homes were regulated with conditional use permits. "It practically guaranteed everyone would show up to oppose them."

Case law generally upheld those trying to keep group living situations out of single-family residential areas. In 1974, in *Belle Terre v. Boraas*, the Supreme Court upheld a city's ordinance defining a family. The opinion stated that equal protection did not apply and that the courts had no reason to interfere with a local jurisdiction's police power. In 1985's *City of Cleburne v. Cleburne Living Center* decision, the Supreme Court acknowledged that the disabled received no special review.

Fair housing rules

The 1988 passage of the Fair Housing Amendments Act forced

courts and local governments to treat the disabled differently. The law added the disabled to its existing list of protected classes. Under the act, the broad definition of "handicap" extends to alcohol or drug addiction. However, the law excludes residents "whose tenancy would constitute a direct threat to the health and safety of other individuals." The Kansas supreme court ruled last April that Leavenworth County, near Kansas City, could prohibit the operation of a group home for high-risk sex offenders who are elderly and disabled (News, August/September 2006).

The FHAA also required that cities whose zoning law did not limit the number of unrelated people that could live in a single-family residence allow group homes as-of-right. It required those with more restrictive definitions of family to make "reasonable accommodations" for homes housing the disabled. Seven years later, in *Edmonds v. Oxford House*, the Supreme Court upheld the FHAA and established that local laws that define families in a way that excludes group homes are not exempt from the law.

Experts like Lauber say the government had good reason to force cities to approach community residences more like families and less like institutions. He cites over 100 studies that show that community residences have little impact on property values, as long as group homes are not clustered on one block. Jaffe points out that traffic and congestion, often a top concern of low-density neighborhoods, are also likely to have a minimal impact because few residents own vehicles.

Many cities have stopped regulating group homes altogether. "The pendulum swung way far the other way," says Eric King, the community residential siting coordinator for the Portland, Oregon, Office of Neighborhood Involvement. King says Portland amended its code in the early 1990s to allow group homes in any residential district.

"Things got sited anywhere, without any process," King says. As a result, new problems began to occur: The lack of regulations allowed providers to cluster homes in certain neighborhoods. Neighbors armed with negative stereotypes stormed city hall looking for recourse.

Something similar was happening in Milwaukee. Until this year, the city mandated that group homes must be at least 2,500 feet apart. As more and more community residences came into the city, that requirement was largely ignored. Alderman Joe

Davis led an effort to map community residences and found a disproportionate number of the facilities in his northwestern district. "Literally, one would be approved on one block and then another would apply for the same block," creating concerns among families about neighborhood instability, Davis says. Group home advocates are trying to abolish both the city law and a similar state statute.

Portland's solution was the creation of the Community Residence Siting program, which applies conflict dispute resolution tactics to group home sitings that stir discontent among neighbors. The program identifies community leaders and brings them together with care providers to map out a public involvement process, with the city office as a mediator. King says the mediation has paid off. "We don't have people screaming at elected officials anymore," he says.

Jaffe, meanwhile, isn't afraid to say that the best place for many group homes, especially larger ones, may be in multifamily zones, where amenities like shopping and transportation are more likely to be within easy walking distance.

Tim Sullivan

Sullivan is a freelance writer in Oakland, California. This article was published in January 2007.

Resources

Reading. "The Impact of Residency Restrictions on Sex Offenders and Correctional Management Practices: A Literature Review" is a 2006 study prepared for the California Research Bureau. The 2004 study "Sex Offender Recidivism: A Simple Question" is available at www.psepc-sppcc.gc.ca/publications/corrections/200403-2_e.asp.

Online. The Association for the Treatment of Sexual Abusers is at www.atsa.com. The Center for Sex Offender Management: www.csom.org. The California Coalition Against Sexual Assault: www.calcasa.org.

THE SHOCK OF THE NEW

Lewiston, Maine, learns how to treat Somali immigrants like anyone else in town.

Peter Blais

Two visitors sheepishly stepped back off the rug and waited in the doorway of the Somali storefront mosque in downtown Lewiston, Maine. hey had inadvertently broken a Muslim custom by failing to remove their footwear before entering a place of worship. Such clumsy moments have been inevitable for the longtime citizens of this small central Maine city of roughly 36,000 people and 1,100 Somali refugees who have moved here in the past year and a half. Dealing with the unexpected influx of new citizens from a vastly different culture has been an ongoing challenge for local officials and residents alike.

Newcomers

Many Somalis have fled their native land in recent years due to civil unrest and famine. The U.S., like other United Nations member countries, accepts a limited number of refugees for permanent resettlement. Many of these "primary refugees" originally settled in large cities, including Atlanta, Chicago, and Nashville. Unhappy with the crime, housing, schools, and lack of employment in those larger cities, many Somalis began looking for other places to live. Affordable housing, safe neighborhoods, and potential employment made Lewiston an attractive place for many to resettle as "secondary refugees."

Large numbers of Somalis first began moving to Lewiston in February 2001. According to assistant city administrator Phil Nadeau, 20 to 30 families a month began relocating to this former mill town, located along the banks of the Androscoggin River. By late summer 2002, an estimated 1,100 Somalis, representing better than three percent of the city's population, had made Lewiston their new home.

This tidal wave of new citizens challenged the largely homogeneous municipality, which was battling economic woes and a declining population base (down from a high of about 42,000 in the late 1970s to 35,690 in 2000). With a $900 million state deficit and a $200 billion federal shortfall in the offing, city officials wondered whether they could count on continued state and federal funding to help meet the Somalis' social service needs.

According to Nadeau, programs and services for immigrants, most of whom are Somali, added $382,000 to the fiscal 2003 municipal budget, mainly for extra costs for the Office of General Assistance and for English as a Second Language (ESL) programs. That sum represented about one percent of the $40 million raised through local property taxes for the year. The remaining $30 million needed to cover the city's annual budget of $70 million came from local fees and state and federal funds.

In October, financial pressures, coupled with some confrontations between newcomers and long-time residents, prompted Mayor Laurier Raymond to send a letter to Somali elders asking them to slow the migration of Somalis into the city. The letter angered Somali elders, who requested special police protection for their people.

The resulting national media attention cast the city in a negative light, prompting the mayor to apologize for any misunderstandings his letter may have caused. More recently, hard feelings seem to have been put aside and city officials are doing the work needed to meet the needs of its newest citizens.

Practical steps

City planning director James Lysen, AICP, says it soon became apparent to Lewiston officials that the resources for secondary refugees were less than those for primary refugees. Primary refugees—those coming directly from their native land—are eligible for substantial federal assistance, and the federal government takes the lead in administering the programs and resettling families.

The federal limit is 70,000 primary refugees per year nationwide. Maine's annual allotment is about 250. Most of Maine's primary refugees have resettled in the state's largest city, Portland, located 40 miles south of Lewiston. Four primary refugee families settled in Lewiston in 2000.

Many recent Somali refugees reaching Lewiston have been secondary refugees, those who left their original U.S. city for another. Fewer federal dollars are available for them; their social needs must be met mainly with state, local, and nonprofit dollars. "Unfortunately, we had no knowledge of this process before it started happening," Lysen says.

City planners, Lysen says, had to come to grips with some important needs of both refugees and city staff in order to better serve the Somali immigrants. These include:

• Cultural education of staff and residents. Unfamiliar with Somali culture, Lewiston residents were taken aback by such everyday Somali customs as bargaining for goods and services and the religious act of washing their feet many times a day.

When Somalis obtained zoning permits and opened a "market," planners were surprised to discover a butcher shop there. "We didn't understand their concept of a market, and they didn't know that our regulations about hygiene and food handling are much different than those in Africa," Lysen says. "We just didn't know the questions to ask or have a clear understanding of what a 'market' was to them. Being educated about those types of cultural differences is helpful."

• Better informing local officials about how to deal with potential problems and develop solutions. The Carter administration established the original refugee resettlement programs in the late 1970s, Lysen says. That initiative designated nonprofit organizations to manage resettlement programs. The process essentially bypassed local and state governments.

But local people tend to approach local officials first. "Community officials need to be informed early on about what's going on so they can address the concerns of their constituency," Lysen says. Also, elected officials are the ones making decisions on budgetary items such as general assistance or English as a Second Language programs.

• Identifying nonprofit agencies willing to assist refugee groups with employment training, health care, and other issues. Lysen says a new group called the United Somali Women of Maine (USWM) is working closely with Community Concepts, a health care and housing advocacy group. Community Concepts has provided office space for USWM, offered USWM members the opportunity to serve on Community Concepts' board of directors, and allocated $20,000 in grant money for the Somali immigrants.

Lysen notes that St. Mary's Hospital, Bates College, Coastal Enterprises, and other nonprofit agencies have gotten involved in funding housing, business start-ups, and other programs.

• Setting up new programs so they are adaptable to different ethnic groups. Many of Lewiston's Hispanic immigrants have the same needs as the Somalis and are benefiting from some of the programs devised since the Somalis' arrival.

• Developing different types of programs. Every new arrival doesn't need to be immersed in a full-blown ESL program. By targeting some ESL programs to the workplace, new employees can quickly master the 60 or so words they may need to know to perform a certain job, rather than the thousands of words needed to function in society. Successful workplace ESL programs have been developed by the University of Maine and used in several Maine cities, including Lewiston.

• Dealing with cultural differences in the workplace to improve employee retention rates. Somalis have been fired for sending their brothers to work for them for a day, a common practice in Somalia but generally taboo in the U.S. Lysen also notes that many Somali refugees are surprised at the fast pace of life here. "Cultural education needs to work both ways," Lysen advises. "We need to know about them, and they need to know about us."

• Accommodating new housing needs. Many Somalis have large, extended families and often seek six- and seven-bedroom apartments to house family members. It's been a struggle to locate apartments that large, and the city has encouraged redevelopment of existing apartments into larger units. "That's a housing issue. Planners need to understand they can have an impact on meeting those needs," Lysen says.

• How public transportation affects employment. Many Somalis have rented apartments and found employment in downtown Lewiston, which is ideal for those unused to owning automobiles and willing to walk to work and services. However, it has been a challenge for those living in more outlying parts of the city.

Figure 2-10 Participants in a community friendship walk held in Lewiston in October 2002, shortly after the city's mayor asked Somali leaders to help slow down the pace of immigration there. Source: Laura Segall, Lewistown Sun Journal

"The limited public transportation within our community, and the fact many Somalis work second shift when buses don't run, have been major roadblocks to their gaining employment," Lysen says. "We have a limited bus route in Lewiston. We're working on these issues now, but having a heads-up earlier [about the need to expand public transportation] would have helped."

• Figuring out who the immigrant leaders are. Lewiston officials first tried to approach elders and those who spoke English when seeking out community leaders. "You tend to think of Somalis as a homogeneous group," Lysen says. "But, in fact, there are many clans. One person may not speak for all the clans. We had to learn about the structure of their society and who the leaders really were."

• Employee testing may not always be appropriate. Standard employee tests measure basic reading, writing and arithmetic skills. But because of the language barrier, some Somalis had problems passing these tests and were denied jobs. A local bakery trained Somalis to do certain tasks and they performed well. But when the employer administered the standardized tests, several Somalis failed and were denied employment. "We realized that with some employers and employees the tests might not be appropriate," Lysen says.

• Refugees have a right to interpretive services. Communities dealing with federal money and requirements must provide interpreters when needed. Lewiston officials had to learn how to access interpretation services.

In December, Lewiston hired Victoria Scott as full-time immigrant refugee programs manager. Scott will assist Nadeau in dealing with the multiple state, federal, and nonprofit agencies taking part in Lewiston's Somalian resettlement effort.

"The most important issue is community involvement," Scott says. Without that, it is very difficult to have successful integration, she adds. Scott also emphasizes the importance of involving the community's younger residents. "It's tough to change attitudes and perceptions of parents," she says. "But dealing with youths in and outside of schools can be a very important component."

Recent events

The number of new Somalian arrivals has dropped since August, down from as many as 60 individuals per month through the first eight months of 2002 to a couple dozen total from September through December. Nadeau attributes the slowdown to the beginning of the school year; the September 11 anniversary, which dampened movement around the country of American Muslims concerned for their personal safety; and the national attention the city received. Meanwhile, Lewiston is gearing up for an ongoing shift in its population.

"We may have to staff up a few positions to deal with case loads," Nadeau says. "But that's a moving target. We're doing everything we can to use existing capacity that's out there within state organizations and nonprofits. We've done that on multiple levels—housing, job retraining, adult education, ESL, K–12 programs, curriculum changes in the school department, agricultural initiatives in an urban environment."

He adds: "The wonderful part of these initiatives, like the agricultural and affordable housing initiatives, is that they will have spill-over benefits to other populations that have nothing to do with immigration and refugee resettlement."

What's ahead

Lewiston is experiencing what University of Northern Iowa researcher Mark Gray calls "sudden ethnic diversification." In response, Nadeau and city administrator Jim Bennett are working on a strategy that would allow all city departments to respond over the long haul.

A formal strategy for dealing with people isn't the same as dealing with other processes, Nadeau says. "When you build a road you know you're going to have to deal with permitting, facilities, compaction, and road-base levels," he notes. "You also have to go to the neighborhoods, talk to people, and go through the political process. There's an automatic feature to it. Everyone knows the steps."

It would be ideal, he says, to reach a similar intuitive level with refugee resettlement, "so that all the steps are well known and everything you do is part of the normal process." Dealing with refugees has to be reflected in policies, ordinances, and zoning, he adds. "You want to incorporate what is going on with the changing cultural and ethnic make-up of your community and express that as part of your strategic and comprehensive plan."

In an uncertain world, refugee resettlement is likely to be part of the American landscape for years to come. Can other communities learn from Lewiston's experience?

"Lewiston is not so unique that a similar set of circumstances couldn't develop someplace else," Nadeau says. "With improvements in technology, mobile communications, and transportation, we've created an environment in which the sudden movement of people can occur more easily. Lewiston will be a model for other communities that may encounter similar circumstances."

Peter Blais is a freelance writer and media consultant who lives in North Yarmouth, Maine. This article was published in February 2003.

Lewiston and Portland Team Up

Seeking a creative way to handle an influx of Somali refugees, Portland and Lewiston—Maine's two largest cities—joined forces in September 2001 to apply for Unexpected Arrivals Grant (UAG) funds from the federal Office of Refugee Resettlement. "We work in our own communities, but we also support one another," says Portland-based Cheryl Hamilton, program supervisor for the Portland and Lewiston Refugee Collaborative.

Somali secondary refugees began arriving in Portland two years ago. But Portland has a serious shortage of affordable housing. Lewiston, 40 miles north, has a larger supply. Work-

ing with a Portland case manager, a few Somali families living
in Portland's family shelter relocated to Lewiston in 2001. Soon
the two communities decided to apply jointly for the UAG
funds. "We applied for $500,000 and received $265,000, to be
split between the two municipalities over 18 months," Hamilton
explains.

Portland's share was allocated to its social services division.
Lewiston's went to its general assistance office. The original
grant enabled both cities to hire their own case managers as well
as a shared account clerk and a shared cultural skills trainer.

The UAG program's purpose is to help resettle secondary
migrants, assist with their immediate needs, and provide some
long-term care assistance, Hamilton notes. When a family ar-
rives, she explains, its first point of entry is the general assistance
office in both communities. Their next stop is a case manager,
who helps them connect with schools, jobs, and social services.

Officials in the two cities expected to work with 1,000 refugees
over 18 months. Because of the larger than expected migration to
Lewiston and a continued migration to Portland, that number arrived within the first nine months of the grant period. Recently,
the two cities received a supplemental grant of $216,000. The
extra funds enabled the communities to hire seven staff people:
two case managers and an employment counselor in each city
plus a shared program supervisor.

"One of the biggest challenges has been employment," Hamilton says. "We've partnered with the local career centers in Portland and Lewiston to house our employment counselors at their
sites. Having the employment counselors at the career centers,
rather than city hall, is important because we want to mainstream the refugees and integrate them into the community."

The collaborative also hosts monthly diversity workshops in
both cities. Attendees include those who come into contact with
the refugees: social workers, police officers, nurses, librarians. As
many as 100 individuals have attended a single session.

"Many municipalities create new agencies to help a targeted
population," Hamilton says. "But secondary refugees should be
treated like anyone else who moves to town. You can develop
services to serve them rather than create new social service agencies."

CHAPTER

3

The Jobless

In the U.S., to be officially unemployed is to be in a somewhat privileged position—at least compared to people who have been jobless for more than six months or who find themselves permanently outside the workforce. That's because those who are officially unemployed qualify for government benefits and others do not.

Day laborers do not meet the definition. They are always seeking work but can never be officially unemployed. And then there are workers who cannot find work or have given up the search.

Experts have estimated that when the official unemployment rate was 5.5 percent in 2004, there was an "unofficial employment rate" of 15.2 percent. Further, researchers have found that unemployment is linked to higher suicide rates, declining health, more divorces, increased depression and stress, and increased crime and social violence.

Some additional statistics emerged at the end of 2007. According to the U.S. Department of Agriculture, the number of households who got food from food banks and other community sources rose by 26 percent between 2001 and 2006. Some of those seeking help were working but homeless, unable to meet their basic needs.

At the same time, the food pantries were reporting shortages—partly because of declining donations from restaurants and the federal government.

Figure 3-1
A hiring area in Laguna Beach. Source: Stacy Harwood

ALL IN A DAY'S WORK

Day laborers create challenges for municipalities across the U.S.

By David Downey

It is a scene repeated daily on street corners and in parking lots throughout the U.S.: Dozens of people wait for homeowners and building contractors to sweep by and offer a day's work. Dressed in faded blue jeans and paint-blotched sweatshirts, they look for an opportunity to paint houses or mow backyards, to pound nails or pour concrete.

The so-called day laborers—the vast majority of them men—rush forward as a sport utility vehicle or truck pulls up. They swarm around it, knowing that in a matter of seconds they could be on the way to earning up to $100 for a day's work.

The scene may not make sense to Americans who hold down regular jobs. For men like 23-year-old Jose Delgadillo, it makes perfect sense.

Delgadillo says he is building a three-bedroom house for his wife and baby girl in Mexicali, Mexico, just south of the international border. He says he can find work in his hometown, but the pay is too low to cover his costs. "The pay in Mexicali is $10 or $12 per day," Delgadillo says. "Here, that's for one hour."

So, for a few months at a time, he heads north into California to stay with his sister in the Riverside area and picks up day jobs from customers leaving the parking lot of the local Home Depot. "I need the money for my house, for my family," says Delgadillo. "I need to work." Delgadillo often pulls in $80 to $100 a day. Of that, he sends $20 to $30 to his wife.

Big supply

On any given day, close to 120,000 laborers congregate at more than 400 locations in nearly half the states in the U.S. to seek work as construction workers, landscapers, painters, roofers, and drywall installers, according to the first comprehensive national study on the phenomenon, released in January.

Homeowners who want work done around the house represent 49 percent of the employers, the study found. Contractors in search of cheap labor hire another 43 percent.

Although there are regional differences when it comes to wages—employers on the West and East coasts tend to pay a couple of dollars more than those in the nation's interior—the mean hourly wage is $10, says Abel Valenzuela, Jr., director of the Center for the Study of Urban Poverty at the University of California, Los Angeles, and one of the nation's foremost experts on the issue. "Most workers go out for about $100 a day," Valenzuela says.

Valenzuela teamed up on the study with researchers Nik Theodore from the Center for Urban Economic Development at the University of Illinois at Chicago and Edwin Melendez at the Milano Graduate School of Management and Urban Policy at the New School University. The study is "On the Corner: Day Labor in the U.S."

The researchers found wide fluctuations in job availability. As a result, monthly earnings vary from $500 to $1,400 a month. At best, a laborer earns $15,000 in a year—at about the federal poverty level for a family of three, Valenzuela says.

Close-up

Who are those people standing on street corners waiting for a day job? Valenzuela and the study's coauthors estimate that 59 percent were born in Mexico and 28 percent in Central America. The next largest group, totaling seven percent, was born in the U.S.

The researchers found that three-quarters of the day laborers lack papers authorizing them to live or work in this country. Opponents of illegal immigration say the throngs of day laborers reflect the federal government's failure to protect its borders. By some estimates, as many as 11 million people are in the U.S. illegally.

Valenzuela says the root causes of the day laborer phenomenon run far deeper. There is much more reliance today on part-time, self-employed, and contractual workers than there was 20 years ago, he says. "Day labor is at the bottom of this changing structure of the economy," Valenzuela says. "Day laborers are similar to substitute teachers. They try to get a job every day, and some days they are called for work and some days they are not."

The rise of day labor also stems from economic pressures in the construction industry. Many smaller contractors try to hold down costs by hiring temporary, nonunion labor. And then there is the do-it-yourself movement, which has emboldened homeowners to tackle their own projects—with a little help from day laborers, Valenzuela says.

In short, day labor is not just about people crossing the border. It is supply and demand in the workplace. "I firmly believe that if we had no immigration we would still see day laborers," Valenzuela says.

Concentrations

Day laborers are in demand all over the U.S., but according to the study, 60 percent of them can be found on the West Coast and in the Southwest.

Valenzuela reports vast numbers in California, Arizona, Texas, Oregon, and Washington. The six largest concentrations are in the metropolitan areas of Los Angeles, New York City, San Francisco, San Diego, Atlanta, and Washington, D.C., in that order, he says.

Communities in those regions have been among the most active in trying to move laborers off the street.

Some laborers have been observed congregating behind buildings and urinating in bushes, says Michael O'Reilly, mayor of Herndon, Virginia (pop. 23,000), about 20 miles west of Washington, D.C. When employers are slow in arriving some mornings, some laborers go inside the nearest convenience store to buy beer and drink on the sidewalk, he says.

*Figure 3-2
The Laguna
Beach facility.
Source: Stacy
Harwood*

Laborers are also accused of committing crimes, but those accusations are often based on a false stereotype, says Lynn Svensson, director for the San Diego-based Day Labor Research Institute. "Day laborers don't commit more crimes than other groups," Svensson says. "While anti-immigrant groups love to portray day laborers as 'illegal' immigrants, implying that illegal means criminal, the evidence is not there to support this notion."

In most cases, says O'Reilly, people are simply unnerved at the sight of a crowd. "If there were 80 to 100 of any type of people standing on the street corner, there would be concern," O'Reilly says. "You'd think, 'What are they up to?'"

Some communities have tried to disperse the crowds by passing anti-loitering and anti-solicitation ordinances, only to find the laborers reappearing elsewhere. Many have been told their measures are unconstitutional and that laborers have a right to stand on the sidewalk and speak to someone about a job.

Hiring halls

A number of cities are trying a new strategy. They have established hiring halls that provide a formal venue for employer and worker to meet. Such centers, while far from perfect, also have improved conditions for laborers, Valenzuela says.

The study found that those who secure work in the streets may be abused. Nearly half at times are not paid the promised amount after completing a task. Forty-four percent have been denied water or food breaks. One-fifth have suffered a work-related injury.

At the time of the national study, conducted in late 2004, researchers counted 63 worker centers in 17 states. About one in five laborers nationwide is now finding work through these centers, the study estimates. Valenzuela notes, however, that the centers have not had much time to establish a track record. Most have existed only since 2000.

Los Angeles takes the lead

Los Angeles is widely credited with creating the first such worker center—opened in 1989 in L.A.'s Harbor City area—and with currently operating the most comprehensive day labor program in the U.S. Delphia Jones, who directs the city's human services and family development division within the Community Development Department, says Los Angeles runs seven centers and is preparing to open four more by year's end. That is far more than any other city.

The Los Angeles centers are generally open daily 6 a.m. to 2:30 p.m. Laborers and employers sign in as they arrive. Laborers write down their skills and prospective employers record what tasks they need to complete. Jobs are assigned through a lottery system, Jones says.

Mike Hernandez, a former city council member and currently assistant chief of staff for council members Jan Perry and Bernard Parks, played a key role in setting up several centers in the 1990s. "We try to make sure there is an orderly dispensing of jobs," he says of the lottery system. "But at the same time, we are not going to force the customers to take someone they don't want."

Most Los Angeles centers operate out of trailers, Jones says, although the one in Cypress Park is located in a permanent building. The centers have seating areas, bathrooms, and, in some cases, space for English and computer classes. Most have computers that laborers can use to look for jobs.

Jones says the city works closely with neighborhood leaders and home improvement stores to establish employment centers. In some cases, the hiring hall shares a parking lot with a home improvement store. The exception is in downtown Los Angeles, where the center is located in the city's fashion district, she says.

The city-funded centers are operated by nonprofit groups, Jones says. They include the Youth Policy Institute, the Central American Resource Center, and Instituto de Educacion Popular del Sur de California.

Figure 3-3 Contractors are asked to support a hiring service in Laguna Beach. Source: Stacy Harwood

Says Valenzuela: "Los Angeles is probably the model of how to work with different community stakeholders, including the workers, the employers, the police, merchants, residents, elected officials, city planning agencies, and increasingly, home improvement stores. Everybody else is trying to catch up."

Facing setbacks

Los Angeles has succeeded in moving most laborers off the street corner and out of the home improvement store parking lot, city officials say. But there have been setbacks.

In 2004, laborers began to congregate around a home improvement store near Cypress Park. Vendors were selling food in the store parking lot and attracting crowds of store customers, Hernandez says, and those crowds were attracting hordes of laborers. The city and store worked together to eliminate the attraction, he says.

The city of Los Angeles spends $1.7 million a year on its seven hiring halls, Jones says. To date, most of the costs have been met by federal community development block grant funds, she says, but the city also has tapped its general fund.

Now the city is seeking a more reliable funding source. The city council is studying the option of requiring all new home improvement stores to mitigate their community impacts by funding a nearby labor center. "That's about as innovative as it gets," says Valenzuela.

The proposal is also justified, says Jones, because there is a direct link between the presence of home supply stores and the crowds of day laborers. "It's about time that the home improvement stores step up to the plate," Jones says.

Lynn Svensson agrees. "Home Depot-type stores should pay for day labor centers. They are the draw to both employers and day laborers, and have the funds available to pay for them," she says. "What they spend on security guards dedicated only to patrolling the parking lots and chasing off day laborers is equal to the cost of a day labor center."

Home Depot responds

Officials for Home Depot—the nation's second largest retail chain—disagree. They deny that their stores are solely responsible for the crowds that gather near them. "We believe that this isn't a Home Depot issue," says Kathryn Gallagher, a spokeswoman for the chain in Southern California. "This is a complex community issue."

Earlier this year, suburban Burbank became the first city in the nation to require a home supply store to fully fund the operation of a worker center. Roger Baker, AICP, the city's deputy city planner, says the store and center opened simultaneously on January 12.

"We realized that we had a population of temporary workers in that area," Baker says. "We realized that we had no choice but to do something to mitigate the problem."

Burbank required two things of Home Depot: to develop a worker center and to provide money for mitigation. Baker says the mitigation money is not directly linked to the day labor center, but is meant to cover the city's policing, code enforcement, garbage pickup, and other costs associated with the store's operation. However, he says, the Home Depot agreed to put up $94,000 a year for mitigation, and the city secured a contract with Catholic Charities to operate the center for that amount.

The 2,500-square-foot, open-air center is in the store's parking lot. It has restrooms, benches, picnic tables, and awnings. "It has its own independent driveway," Baker says, adding that prospective employers "stop and talk to the person who runs the center and, of course, to the people who are looking for work."

Directly in front of the center, the city painted about 700 feet of curb red both to prevent employers from stopping cars there and to discourage laborers from gathering, Baker says. "The whole point was to get them off the streets and it has worked surprisingly well," he says. "They're inside, it's shaded, and they're off the streets."

While the Burbank project is a first, Gallagher notes that "there have been a few instances in California where the Home Depot was required by local governing agencies to provide space for day labor centers." She adds: "In none of these cases does the Home Depot own or operate the required facilities." The chain operates 1,779 stores nationwide and 198 in California, she says.

Other end of the scale

Not all day labor centers are located down the block or across the street from home improvement stores. Take the one in Herndon, Virginia.

The small, four-square-mile Washington suburb became an East Coast lightning rod in the national debate over illegal immigration when its officials considered what to do about the 100 or so laborers who gathered outside the local 7-Eleven store. Mayor O'Reilly says the town doesn't even have a home improvement store.

After much debate—and loud protest by residents and anti-illegal-immigration activists—the town council chose to set up its own day labor center. The center opened in December in the parking lot of a former police station on the edge of town. It has three paid employees and is run by Project Hope and Harmony, a consortium of faith-based organizations led by Reston Interfaith Inc.

The results have been good so far, says O'Reilly. Only a few people were left standing in front of the 7-Eleven in the middle of winter, he notes.

The center operates on an annual budget of $170,000, provided through a grant from Fairfax County. O'Reilly says the city established a special zoning district for the center. It also passed an ordinance barring anyone from soliciting day jobs anywhere outside the center. O'Reilly says his city was told that an anti-loitering ordinance would not pass constitutional muster but that an anti-solicitation measure would—if laborers had a place where they could exercise their right to free speech.

Legal trouble

The Los Angeles suburb of Glendale is testing that assumption. Glendale's anti-solicitation ordinance was struck down in federal court in May 2005. The city is challenging that ruling in the U.S. Court of Appeals for the Ninth Circuit.

In his 11-page ruling in *Committee of Day Laborers of Glendale v. City of Glendale*, U.S. District Judge S. James Otero said Glendale's ordinance made it unclear where a laborer was supposed to stand. The ordinance states that it is permissible to stand on sidewalks but not on parkways.

"The minute you step in the parkway you violate the ordinance," says Pablo Alvarado, national coordinator for the Los Angeles-based National Day Labor Organization Network. "Obviously, that's not practical for the day laborers."

The city of Glendale says it was not trying to make things difficult. "What we were trying to discourage is the cars illegally stopping in the roadway and the day laborers running from the curb into the streets to try to negotiate a job," says Ann Maurer, senior assistant city attorney. "We're not in any way trying to stop these day laborers from getting work. We're just trying to strike a balance, and so far we have been unable to do so."

Legal questions aside, in some circles Glendale is considered to have one of the nation's better programs. In 1997, the city opened a 6,792-square-foot center designed to accommodate 80 people.

Catholic Charities, the onsite manager, operates out of a trailer. There is outdoor seating and shade for the laborers. There is a drive-through for employers.

But there is no space for classes, says Moises Carrillo, senior supervisor with the city's community development department. The site is designed solely to pair laborers with employers.

The simple approach appears to be working. Carrillo, who earned a master's degree in planning from UCLA, says 70 percent of laborers find work. He attributes that success to the central role the laborers play in the center's operation. A 10-member laborers committee, elected by peers, makes recommendations to the city, he says. The committee can suspend workers for drinking, fighting, using drugs, or venturing back into the street to solicit jobs.

The penalty may be one day, one week, or longer, Carrillo says. But it's always time, never money. "A day off work is hard enough," he says.

When workers go back into the street, it is the laborers on the committee who try to get them back to the center, he says. Not only do they police themselves, but for several years laborers footed half the cost of running the center through $25-a-month dues.

Carrillo reports that the city stopped doing that in July 2005 in the wake of the recent litigation, even though the court ruling didn't bar the practice. Glendale didn't want to give the appearance of putting a price on laborers' right to free speech, he says.

In November, Glendale approved a 2,160-square-foot, $240,445 center expansion that will accommodate up to 150 workers. Construction is scheduled to begin in September.

Getting it right

Laborers also play a high-profile role in managing the First Workers Day Labor Center in central Austin, Texas, says Cecilia Fedorov, spokeswoman for the city's health department. The 5,300-square-foot center, which opened in 1999 in a former Trailways bus depot, is enclosed and air conditioned.

Fedorov says that, on average, 60 percent of the 120 men that come through the center on any given day find work. Austin, which has a recommended minimum wage of $8 an hour, also offers recourse for workers who have been cheated. "The license plate of each employer is written down when they pick up laborers and can be used for future wage claims, if necessary," Fedorov says.

Besides helping to set the ground rules, she says, laborers clean, sweep, and restock paper towels. "It really is their space," Federov says.

Svensson, formerly director of the Glendale center, maintains that Austin and Glendale are successful precisely because laborers help to manage their centers. She also thinks the centers should first focus solely on finding jobs for laborers and only later add job training, computer classes, and counseling.

Alvarado, of the National Day Labor Organizing Network, sharply disagrees. He says that centers offering a multitude of services have also proven adept at landing jobs. He notes that the point of the extra services is to better equip laborers to find what they are looking for.

The opposition

Groups opposed to illegal immigration contend that the centers aggravate the problem of illegal immigration by making it easier for undocumented immigrants to find employment.

Herndon's Mayor O'Reilly says the protesters are missing the point.

"People are dissatisfied with the federal government's response, or lack of response, to illegal immigration and lack of enforcement at the borders, and I understand that," O'Reilly says. "But we can't solve the immigration issue here in our small town of Herndon. We can't close any borders, and we can't issue any guest visas. But if these people are all standing on the corner, we can do something about that."

David Downey is a reporter for the *North County Times* in Escondido, California. This article was published in April 2006.

Best Practices for Day Labor Centers

As communities throughout the U.S. are learning, day labor programs need constant supervision as well as solid measures of success. These measurements include an average rate of employment (a minimum of 80 percent), the number of day laborers left in the street (less than 10 percent of those in the center in the morning), and a drop in complaints about day laborers in the streets (significantly fewer than before the center opens).

Here are some key practices that can assure day labor program success while avoiding common problems:

Limit liability. Although rare, some day laborers going out on jobs have committed crimes. Careful separation of the nonprofit entity that runs the day labor center from the city or county that funds the nonprofit is essential, as is good liability insurance. Even better is nongovernment funding for the center.

Limit the center's services to work. Day laborers are in the streets waiting for work. The main reason they will attend a center and leave the street is for more work at higher wages. To attract more work, use proven, low-cost methods such as passing out flyers at home improvement stores (using day laborer volunteers). Do not offer free food or clothing. Day laborers will quickly abandon a center that looks like a charity. Other services, such as classes, can be added once there is enough work.

Limit participation to day laborers from the immediate area. Opening participation to non-day laborers attracts too many workers; others will take work meant for day laborers, and day laborers will return to the streets. Worse is allowing day laborers from other areas to attend. Word gets out quickly, and the center is flooded with day laborers from other cities.

Monitor surrounding areas. During the center's hours of operation, look for day laborers in the streets, and after hours for drinkers, campers, and the homeless. The center will be blamed for such activities (as will local government).

Practice good discipline and crowd control. All workers should be inside the center at all times. A day labor center should look like any other business from the outside (no workers hanging out). If you have good discipline, the day laborers will respect the program.

Take complaints seriously. Have a formal complaint process. Have complaints written up, and have someone follow up on them.

Make it a "membership" program. Require an application, acceptance into the program, and dues. The application may include photos, an emergency contact in the worker's home country, and fingerprints. Dues—typically $1 per day—have proven to increase participation in day labor programs.

Let day laborers choose the rules and hours of operation. Do not elect a "workers' committee," but rather have day laborers make program decisions during meetings (with an organizer trained in consensus and mediation).

Make sure one key rule is adopted: No members can hang out in the streets. Violation of this rule merits permanent suspension. Other rules: Everyone waits their turn for work, and drinking, drugs, and fights are prohibited.

Day laborers should not choose the director; however, they can and should choose rules and criteria for the director, and should be able to lobby for a replacement.

Limit the staff. The director—the one staff person—supervises the day laborer volunteers and deals with the employers. In addition, an organizer should supervise the staff, receive complaints from the day laborers, and oversee the program (report to the board, write reports, and buy supplies). Day laborers can do all other necessary tasks, including cleanup.

Avoid day labor activists. Activists poison day laborer relations with the police, local government, and the community at large. Skilled in organizing protests, they are also hard to fire.

Create a new nonprofit organization. Social service agencies are not known for efficiency and discipline—the factors most needed for a successful day labor program. With a new nonprofit, you have more control over results. Policies and operations can be designed to avoid problems, and accountability and measures of success can be written into the bylaws.

Lynn Svensson

Svensson is the director of the Day Labor Research Institute, based in San Diego. This article was published in April 2006.

Resources

On the web. Read about "On the Corner: Day Labor in the U.S." at www.sscnet.ucla.edu. Find more about the Day Labor Research Institute at www.daylabor.org. The National Day Labor Organizing Network is at www.ndlon.org. Information about Glendale's program is available at www.ci.glendale. For more on Austin's program, go to www.ci.austin.tx.us.

MUST THE JOBLESS ALSO BE HOPELESS?

**Official unemployment rates may be misleading.
They don't show how joblessness affects communities.**

By David Moberg

Four middle-aged job-seekers sat at a rough wood table on Chicago's West Side talking about why they turned to the nonprofit Michael Barlow Center to help get them back into the workforce. It wouldn't be easy.

All four individuals—three black, one white; two men, two women—had recently been released from prison on charges ranging from theft to first-degree murder. Even before prison, most had experienced long stretches of unemployment, when they supported themselves by stealing jewelry, selling drugs, forgery, and shoplifting, or—for one woman—receiving Aid to Families with Dependent Children. Two had never finished high school. The other two had a smattering of trade school after graduation. Although one man had worked for long stretches as a skilled machinist, the rest had flitted through unstable, low-paid food service, clerical, janitorial, and housekeeping jobs.

They represent one face of the growing problem of long-term joblessness in U.S. But people with much different work and educational histories increasingly endure long stretches of unemployment, even at a time when the official unemployment rate is considered relatively low—at 4.6 percent as of last July.

Many of the long-term unemployed have exemplary work histories, but their jobs have disappeared. David Bevard worked for three decades at the Maytag refrigerator factory in the prairie town of Galesburg, Illinois, where he was president of the local machinists union. When Maytag shut its doors in 2004, moving operations to Mexico and Korea, Bevard helped his 1,600 fellow displaced workers adapt with income support and training funded by the Trade Adjustment Act, the most extensive U.S. program for displaced workers. After that Bevard worked on various union projects and took a part-time auditing job, while drawing early on his pension.

"I've been looking for work since then," he says, "and I'm still looking."

He's frustrated when experts tell him training is the solution. "We've now created a situation where, with free-flowing capital, an entire sector of jobs is disappearing, and nobody knows what's replacing it," he says. "They say wait 10 to 15 years and see, but who can wait?"

Many workers took early retirement packages, as Bevard did, but continued to look for work, says planner Dane Bragg, AICP, Galesburg's current city manager. "Some may choose to work in part-time or service jobs after they take retirement," he notes. "So you have 50-year-old people

Figure 3-4
A carpentry class at St. Leonard's Ministries' Michael Barlow Center in
Chicago. Source: Meghan Stromberg

working at McDonald's. It's very strange. But it has affected the ability of the community to get over the Maytag closing."

David Huber studied computer science at the University of Chicago, steadily getting more responsible and lucrative jobs. Then in 2001, during the nationwide collapse of the high-tech sector, he lost his $160,000-a-year job. Since then he has held only short-term technical jobs at reduced pay with long stretches of unemployment in between. He has often lost out to lower priced foreign workers that companies brought in under the H-1B visa program, which allows employers to fill job shortages with skilled immigrants, including the Indian engineers he helped train to replace him on one job.

"I fully depleted my savings and was nearly homeless on two or three occasions," he says. "On Thanksgiving 2004, I had an apple, baked beans, and water for dinner. Since I could no longer afford my COBRA premiums [to extend his health insurance], I am very fortunate I had no medical emergencies to contend with."

Defining "long term"

The unemployed generally are invisible, even though they regularly make the news. In part, that's because to be counted among the unemployed, someone has to have sought work but not actually worked. Workers are officially counted as "long-term unemployed" when they have been unemployed for six months or more.

But as unemployment drags on, many workers become "discouraged" or "marginally attached" to the workforce, in the language of the Bureau of Labor Statistics. Others settle for part-time work, even though they want a full-time job. Still more involuntarily retire, qualify for Social Security Disability Insurance, or end up in some other government support program. At least part of the prison population could be counted as unemployed, some analysts argue, since poverty or joblessness contributed heavily to their imprisonment.

Using such broad criteria, economist John Schmitt at the Washington-based Center for Economic and Policy Research calculated that when the official unemployment rate was 5.5 percent in 2004, there was an "unofficial employment rate" of 15.2 percent. Most of the increase represents people who had been out of work for a long time.

Even by the official definition, long-term unemployment has increased in recent decades. From the early 1970s to the present, the average duration of unemployment has increased from around 11 to 17 weeks, according to an analysis by the National Employment Law Project, a nonprofit research and advocacy group based in New York.

Usually as a recession ends, employers begin recalling temporarily laid-off workers. But after the recessions of the early 1990s and—even more so—2001, the economy went through a "jobless recovery," in which unemployment continued to grow even after the recessions peaked. Since new jobs on average were not as good as those lost, workers faced a stiffer challenge in finding replacement jobs. And growing numbers of the layoffs during the recession were permanent, as businesses drastically reduced their ranks and shifted more work overseas.

Historically, according to an analysis by the Economic Policy Institute, a leading center for study of labor markets, 10.8 percent of all the unemployed have been out of work more than six months during times when unemployment rates were about 4.7 to five percent. But during the recovery from the 2001 recession, the long-term unemployed constituted 18.4 percent of the unemployed.

"When people lose their jobs, they have a harder, longer road to return to work," says Andrew Stettner, deputy director of the National Employment Law Project. "This is part of the longer term trend that more unemployment comes from permanent layoffs, and people have a harder time finding work of equal value of what they lost."

What's surprising is that long-term unemployment has been rising much faster for white-collar workers, workers with a college education, and experienced workers over 45 years old. In 1989 workers with less than a high school education made up 39.3 percent and college graduates only 9.2 percent of the long-term unemployed. By 2005, those numbers were 24.1 percent and 17 percent, respectively—college graduates nearly doubled their share of long-term unemployment.

Society suffers, too

Long-term unemployment harms workers and society regardless of their education and work history, even if the less-educated, less-skilled, ethnic minority, and lower income workers suffer more. For many years, researchers have found that unemployment is linked to higher suicide rates, declining health, more divorces, increased depression and stress, and increased crime and social violence.

Here's how Montress Greene of Project New Start, a program of the nonprofit North Carolina Rural Economic Development Center that provides training to displaced rural and small-town workers, describes the effects of long-term unemployment on her clients—tobacco processing workers who lost their jobs in rural parts of the state. "Depression, feeling hopeless, escalating family problems, having to move in with relatives, or single mothers going to a shelter. All kinds of things happen to them. It's not a pretty picture."

Society loses, too. First, it loses the production and income the jobless would have generated. But governments and other social institutions pay the widespread costs of coping with the health effects on the jobless (and on those worried about losing a job), combating crime, and losing the social trust societies need.

After the Maytag closing in Galesburg, city revenue stagnated, making it harder to undertake the reinvestment needed for projects such as upgrading the city's water system. But new problems also developed as the workforce and population declined, and median income dropped by roughly 10 percent.

"From the planners' perspective, you hear a lot about unemployment, but where you really see it is in the deterioration of neighborhoods," Bragg says. "We just got information that the teen pregnancy rate ticked up again. Public schools say they see more problems because of less stable environments at home. It just ripples through every facet of the community. And for some reason, everyone looks at the city to solve the problems."

Planner Mike Legg, AICP, now city manager of Kannapolis, South Carolina, saw many of the same effects in 2003, when the closure was announced for the town's major employer, a 5,000-employee textile mill whose previous owners literally owned most of the town.

"All the rest of 2003 and 2004 were a struggle [because of] the social impact of that many people being out of work," Legg says. "Our foreclosure rate went up for the first couple of years. Our food pantries and help agencies really spiked for those first 18 months. Then there were the land-use and long-term economic implications of having the textile mill of that magnitude in the core of the city. What we tried to do as planners was to keep our eyes on the ball—not to try to be everything for everybody, but to diversify the economy, be aggressive about economic development. I can't stress image enough; the last thing we wanted was to be in the spotlight as a dying community."

The growing complexity of long-term unemployment poses challenges about how public policy can best respond. Yet despite their disparate needs, the four ex-offenders, the displaced factory worker, and the jobless high-tech worker introduced earlier need some common social policies.

Above all, one must ask if the nation really wants to reduce unemployment. As economic journalist Louis Uchitelle recounted in his book, *The Disposable American*, since 1979 the U.S. has retreated from the widely accepted, if not always implemented, idea that the federal government should be equally committed to full employment and price stability. Fighting inflation has taken precedence for nearly three decades.

Harvard professor William Julius Wilson, author of *When Work Disappears*, stresses the importance of full employment policies for disadvantaged populations. In the 1990s, there was a sharp drop in the number of people living in areas of concentrated poverty—home to the relatively new "jobless poverty" of the 1970s and 1980s.

"A look at the long-term statistics shows that neither welfare reform nor race-based programs seem to have had much to do with changes in poverty concentration," Wilson writes in a new book on poverty coedited by Sen. John Edwards. Yet even as a booming economy lifted most of the poor, including young black women, one group—young black men—increasingly withdrew from the workforce, too often ending up in the criminal justice system.

Shoring up the middle class

The growing low-skill service sector has absorbed former welfare mothers and reduced long-term unemployment for many low-wage workers. But three million manufacturing jobs vanished from 2000 to 2005, most of them eliminated permanently by technological change, plant closings, and offshoring. These workers typically find it hard to find new jobs that pay anything near to their old wages.

In Kannapolis, Legg says, "the first order of business was to convince former workers that the mill was not coming back." Many workers needed high school degrees and basic problem-solving skills. Many workers with technical skills found jobs in the nearby Charlotte region, and a new outlet mall not far away employed some less-skilled workers. But, Legg says, "Lots are underemployed. They don't have the benefits they had, and they may be working multiple jobs."

From 2001 through 2003, the rate of job displacement from layoff or facility shutdown was the highest since the government first collected data in the 1980s, but by January 2004 only two-thirds of those displaced workers had found jobs, according to a Department of Labor survey. Nearly half of those who found jobs reported lower wages, and one-third took a pay cut of 20 percent or more.

Jobs like those Bevard and Huber had are hard to find, but if they took a Wal-Mart job, they would lose financially and society would lose the productivity of their skills. However, the Bush administration has promoted a "work first" strategy to get people into jobs rapidly, even if more education might pay off better in the long run.

*Figure 3-5
A job-training
center for
the formerly
incarcerated.
Source: Meghan
Stromberg*

More than the usual fiscal and monetary economic stimulus is needed to help such displaced workers. With a large and growing trade deficit, much economic stimulus leaks out to stimulate increased demand for imports, not domestic jobs. Many full-employment advocates argue as well for new rules governing the global economy and policies that directly generate domestic jobs.

But government—through programs such as the Michigan Manufacturing Training Center—can also intervene early to improve the competitiveness of many manufacturers and reduce the risk of dislocation and long-term unemployment. MMTC focuses on bringing state-of-the-art techniques and technology to small- and medium-sized manufacturers.

Other programs involve unions hoping to promote "high road partnerships" with employers to increase skills and productivity, not cut wages or jobs. For example, the Wisconsin AFL-CIO organized, with government and business support, the Wisconsin Regional Training Partnership, which provides training in skilled metalworking for existing job holders, welfare recipients entering the job market, young people, and the long-term un-employed. It also helps businesses work with unions to modernize their technology and work practices.

Many federal initiatives can help long-term unemployed workers, in-cluding insurance and cash payments, regulations, incentives, education and training, labor market information, and social services. But advocates for the unemployed argue that funding—estimated around $30 billion a year—has not kept up with growing needs, especially since the last reces-sion, and the programs are generally far more restrictive and less gener-ous than in other industrial countries.

Figure 3-6
Program participant Johnnie Savory spent 20 years in prison for a crime he says he did not commit. He is now pursuing a degree in criminal justice and petition-ing for clemency. Source: Meghan Stromberg

In the U.S., only about one-third of the unemployed receive unemploy-ment insurance compensation (administered through state governments). Insurance typically lasts 26 weeks, but Congress often extends it during recessions for another 26 weeks. Yet Congress did not renew the extension in 2003, even though it had helped 4.7 million long-term unemployed workers in the previous year and one million workers had already exhausted the extended aid, according to the Center on Budget and Policy Priorities.

For long-term unemployed workers, two of the most important federal initiatives are the Workforce Investment Act, which attempts to coordinate efforts through "one-stop career centers," and the Trade Adjustment Act. The latter provides more generous income support and training than other programs for dislocated workers but only reaches a small fraction of workers displaced by globalization (it only covers workers who produce a product, not service).

Strategies that work—somewhat

There are also local programs to help dislocated workers or disadvantaged long-term unemployed workers. William Schweke, vice president for learning and innovation at the nonprofit CFED (formerly the Corporation for Enterprise Development), reported in "Back on Track: 16 Promising Practices to Help Dislocated Workers, Businesses and Communities" examples of successful state and local programs for dislocated workers that take preventive action, protect living standards, improve connections to employment, enhance workforce skills, and—for a tiny minority—foster entrepreneurial initiative.

In the Pillowtex shutdown, Schweke observed that many state and local government agencies (including the state Department of Commerce and Employment Security Commission), nonprofit groups, the workers' union (UNITE), churches, and community colleges sprang into action. They set up a one-stop center at a Lutheran church near the big mill in Kannapolis and advised workers on resources for emergency needs as well as retraining and extended unemployment benefits available under the Trade Adjustment Act.

Some laid-off workers got jobs in the growing low-wage service economy (such as a nearby outlet mall), and others learned new manual trades or elementary health care work. But by late 2005, when most of the aid and training funds were exhausted, even a flexible, unified, and early response could place only about half the workforce in new jobs.

In Washington State, the labor movement actively participates in the state's dislocated-worker programs and tries to link economic and workforce development. Unions raise questions about the quality of jobs that government aid supports, try to assure that disadvantaged workers have access to jobs at publicly subsidized businesses, and intervene early to find alternatives to plant closings.

Minnesota provides state money to strengthen federal programs and start assistance earlier, reducing the likelihood of lengthy unemployment. "If we can get to workers prior to layoff, it is possible to begin or even complete training before they're unemployed," says Mike Goldman, labor liaison to the state's dislocated worker program. The state Community Stabilization Act requires employers to provide advance notice of layoffs, severance pay, continued health insurance, and other compensation.

But unemployed worker advocates want a TAA that is easier to implement, covers more workers, and provides more income support, which now often ends before training or the job search is complete. Although many workers need help in searching for a job, and such assistance is deemed cost effective, most research supports the value of extended, practical retraining, even for older dislocated workers.

Advocates are split, however, over proposals for wage insurance, which would reimburse workers temporarily for part of the difference between their lost job and a new job. Critics charge that it's just a way to make downward mobility more palatable, not to move workers up in skill and pay.

But there is widespread agreement that even the few existing programs to continue health insurance coverage are ineffective.

Bob Wordlaw, executive director of the Chicago Jobs Council, sees the schools as workers' first chance system—and a system that needs strengthening to keep young people in school and give those not bound for college preparation for skilled work. More than 100 mainly nonprofit groups participate in the council and are part of the second chance system that helps reconnect former workers with the labor force.

Relying on government and foundation funds, some groups provide bridge programs that strengthen basic academic skills and help make people job ready, that is, able to do interviews, dress appropriately, and show up for work regularly. Other programs focus on providing transitional jobs, real but temporary jobs that give people a chance to construct a work history and learn the same basics as in bridge programs.

The Michael Barlow Center, which works with Episcopal-funded residences for men and women ex-offenders, customizes its work for each participant. "Most have burned bridges," says St. Leonard's Ministries executive director Bob Dougherty. "Most are repeat offenders. Many don't have skills. We help them understand what the world of work is like, then give them skills."

While other agencies help with substance abuse problems, the Barlow Center teaches participants marketable skills and how to act at work, then connects the trainees with a job and counsels them for half a year about on-the-job issues. With 300 ex-offenders in related residences and about 200 trainees a year, Dougherty acknowledges that success is elusive. Roughly a fifth of participants end up back in prison, and about 90 a year find jobs. Yet the jobs typically pay poorly and workers "get so discouraged that they fall back into drug patterns," Dougherty says.

Transitional job strategies recognize that many disengaged workers who have long been out of work require more than training, more than job search skills, even more than a job. They need support and guidance as they try to establish themselves in the world of work.

"The essence of the program is building a work history, to make people more marketable and a less risky hire," says Amy Rynell, a researcher for the Chicago-based Heartland Alliance, a leader in a national network of 200 transitional jobs programs. "We test and train the employee, not on the employer's dollar, as a way to win over employers."

Darla Riley, 56, a former bookkeeper who dropped out of work to raise her daughter for 10 years on income from AFDC, turned to Heartland to help her find a job so that she could qualify for new mixed income housing that was replacing her aging public housing. Already Heartland has helped her find three jobs, and now it is providing training to help replace a job she had to quit due to injury.

With tears of joy at her new home and with fear that she might return to living conditions she once had, Riley is still in transition to a stable working life. "The only thing that keeps me full of faith," she says, "is that Heartland is here for me."

As long-term unemployment becomes a greater problem for more American workers, the country will need to turn to new national policies—such as a full employment economy, national health insurance, and a more worker-oriented approach to globalization. It will also need to fund more generously and make more comprehensive the wide variety of programs that serve as intermediaries between discouraged workers and future jobs. But first it will have to recognize the personal and social costs of long-term unemployment.

"It's very easy for long-term unemployment to fall out of sight," says Anne Bacon, senior director of workforce development for The Rural Center in North Carolina. "People in need just get used to lower standards of living. If we paid more attention, maybe it wouldn't be the case."

David Moberg is a senior editor at *In These Times,* a national news magazine. This article was published in October 2007.

4

Poor Communities

Some problems are so entrenched that they have lasted for generations. In the U.S., the rural poor have always been a fixture in the popular imagination. Today, about 15 percent of rural Americans actually live in poverty. Likewise, victims of environmental injustice have drawn national attention for decades.

Laws and demographics change, however, and living conditions may change as a result. Rural communities within easy commuting distance of cities have tended to grow and prosper during the last several decades. Industry, government, and planners have added environmental justice to their agendas. Industrial polluters have been fined and families compensated for the damage they have suffered.

Native Americans are also making a notable turnaround—partly because federal law now allows tribes to provide services to their own members. Many tribes have thrived by opening casinos and other businesses. Still, taken as a group, Native Americans lag behind the U.S. average on almost every socioeconomic measure, including median household income, child poverty, unemployment, and infant mortality.

Figure 4-1
One in seven rural Americans lives in poverty, often because wages are relatively low in jobs like farm work, fishing, and meat processing. Source: © iStock-
photo.com/Glenn Frank

WHERE PROBLEMS PERSIST

One-sixth of the nation is rural—and many rural residents are needy.

By Mark B. Lapping

Rural America has experienced many profound changes. First Majority-Last Minority, John Shover's 1976 history of rural life in the U.S., encapsulates the stark differences between the beginning of the 20th century and the beginning of the 21st. The vast majority of Americans once lived in the open countryside, and villages and hamlets dotted the landscape; now rural residents constitute about one-sixth of the population. Still, this amounts to better than 50 million people.

Often stereotyped, ignored, or simply forgotten, rural Americans face a number of vexing and seemingly intractable problems and challenges. Those who live in rural places are among the poorest, least well provided for—in terms of access to human, educational, social, and health care services—and most inadequately housed of all Americans. They face a deficit of federal support, at least relative to urban and suburban Americans, and policy initiatives directed towards their needs are scant, poorly defined, and often poorly delivered.

With dwindling economic opportunities and the decline in traditional occupations like farming, forestry, mining, and fishing as well as manufacturing, the prospects for many rural communities look rather bleak.

Why is rural America overlooked?

The answer to this question is rather complex. First, the media too rarely cover events and issues in rural areas. And when there is coverage, the events tend to be tragic, like a mine disaster in West Virginia or the leveling of Greensburg, Kansas. Oriented as they are to major metropolitan markets, the media just don't see the triumphs and travails of everyday life on Main Street.

Second, Americans see rural people through stereotypical lenses. Rural people either are characters out of Deliverance or Mayberry R.F.D.—outright depravity and social disintegration on the one hand or overly romanticized folksiness and neo-Jeffersonian virtue on the other.

Another stereotype is that most rural Americans are farmers. In fact, with less than two percent of the entire U.S. population engaged in agriculture, farming occupies an ever smaller niche in our rural economy. The diversity of lived experience in rural places is immense. Yet the myth persists—and it does enormous harm to rural Americans, particularly when federal policy and programs are involved.

Third is the issue of invisibility. Much of rural America is flyover country. Intellectuals and cultural critics often dismiss country people and places as conservative, religiously and socially fundamentalist, backward, and worse.

Finally, even among planners and other professionals, there appears to be a sense that rural problems can be solved by "thinking small." The really big problems, as well as the solutions, lie elsewhere.

Who are rural Americans?

Different definitions of what constitutes "rural" have long plagued the discussion of rural problems and policies. Suffice it to say that today the U.S. Census Bureau has categorized close to three-quarters of all counties in the nation as rural. Complicating the picture further is the fact many places that were considered distinctly rural some years ago may now be little more than suburbs caught in the midst of metropolitan sprawl.

Further, communities that existed a century ago may have disappeared. For the most part, the nation's rural population has been in steady decline since 1900, and ghost towns can be found in every region of the nation.

Yet there have also been several instances of rural turnaround. Even today, some rural areas such as southern Oregon, mid-coast Maine, and western North Carolina, are experiencing substantial population growth. Such places are not evenly distributed across the country, however. Large parts of the Great Plains continue to decline as the overall population ages, agriculture requires less labor, and young people move elsewhere.

Rural communities within easy commuting distance of cities and their more robust and diversified economies have tended to grow during the last several decades, regardless of region. The same is true of communities on the interstate highway system and those with amenities: water, recreational opportunities, and aesthetically pleasing environments. For various reasons, growth has come to the Upper Great Lakes, the Pacific Northwest, the Mountain West, parts of the South, and some portions of New England.

Some of this growth has been fueled by the retirement choices of the early baby boomers and by technological and communications advances that have made working in rural areas and small towns more feasible. Americans tend to idealize small towns as the very best locations for raising families and this, no doubt, has contributed to the rural growth that is occurring.

Racial and ethnic diversity has increased in rural America, though not in every community. Traditionally, the vast majority of rural African Americans lives in the "Black Belt" of the Deep South. This continues to be the case, with nearly four out of five rural blacks currently living in this region.

In addition, the rural Hispanic population is growing—and not only along the nation's southern border. Attracted by economic opportunities in manufacturing, meatpacking, and construction, rural Latinos have been expanding into new regions. In fact, rural Hispanic population growth has been greater than its urban counterpart during the last decade or so.

Likewise, immigrants are a growing part of our rural population. In a good number of rural counties, the foreign born constitute more than five percent of the local population. This is a relatively new component of the non-metro population base.

Although their numbers have grown modestly in the past few decades, non-Hispanic whites still constitute the largest proportion of the nation's rural population, especially in Appalachia, the Mountain West, northern New England, the Upper Great Plains, and the Ozarks. This group also has the highest percentage of elderly. Indeed, rural America is aging more than metro counties are not only because of the migration of retirees to the country but also as the result of the continuing out-migration of young adults in their child-rearing years.

A disproportionate number of the elderly are women, mostly because they tend to live longer. As rural America ages, new challenges to provide both formal and informal services to this part of the population will mount. The aging of the rural population is certainly not without its benefits, however, because older Americans bring capital such as pensions and Social Security payments into the local economy, and they require services, such as health care, that can provide necessary employment.

In Indian country, which contains many of the nation's poorest counties, the population has shown only modest growth. About half of all Native Americans live in rural places, where the largest number of reservations is located. Compared with the rest of the population, rural Native Americans fare the worst in terms of income, educational attainment, health status, chronic unemployment, and overall poverty rates.

The enduring legacy

Perhaps the greatest single challenge confronting rural America is the chronic, grinding poverty that has gripped rural areas and small towns for decades. Approximately one in seven rural Americans lives in poverty, and poverty rates there have consistently been higher than in urban areas. Consider that the percentage of rural people to urban people who depended on federal food stamps was 7.5 percent versus 4.8 percent in 2001. This gulf has been widening over the last several years. By 2006 the rural dependency on food stamps rose to 10 percent of all rural residents while the urban rate grew to seven percent.

Rural poverty is felt most acutely by the young, the disabled, and the elderly, society's most vulnerable populations. Between 2000 and 2006, the percentage of rural children living at or below the official poverty level increased in the great majority of the states. Maine, not always thought of as a poor rural state, showed the largest percentage increase in children in rural poverty, with a rise of more than seven percent.

And while only a quarter of the rural population is composed of children, in 2001 they accounted for 43 percent of all food stamp recipients.

Traditionally, poor rural areas include the Black Belt of the Deep South, Appalachia, portions of the Great Plains, especially where Native American reservations are located, and areas of the Southwest, also a region where many rural Native Americans and Latinos are heavily represented. Compared to metropolitan areas, rural or non-metro poverty affects a greater percentage of the total population and is more often multigenerational or chronic.

Long-standing poverty rates may have declined over recent years in some parts of rural America, but in those counties classified as "persistently poor" by the U.S. Census, the poor may constitute as much as 60 percent of the total local population base. Very high unemployment, low rates of educational attainment, a high percentage of female-headed households, and other markers of poverty continue to plague whole regions across the nation.

Possible causes

In her book *Poverty Knowledge*, published in 2001, researcher Alice O'Connor provides a marvelous survey of how policy makers and researchers have conceived of poverty, its causes, consequences, and solutions in modern America. Many have historically seen the causes of poverty as either people-based—"the culture of poverty"—or place-based, such as the Deep South's institutionalization and persistence of racism. For rural areas both perspectives seem relevant.

A social system that conflates race and class has certainly been in effect throughout the nation. Likewise, the realities of rural labor markets and employment patterns tend to reinforce low-wage jobs, especially when educational levels are low. Because there are relatively few employment opportunities in rural places, there is also minimal competition for labor, which keeps wages and benefits flat. Often, too, a single industry or a dominant employer will restrict job options in rural communities.

The rise of globalization over the last few decades has also played a role in deepening rural poverty in that jobs previously located in rural communities, including light and low-tech manufacturing, have been sent to lower wage regions of the world. The aging of so much of the rural population, together with the growth in single-parent and single-person households, low educational achievement, poor health status, limited availability of social and other human services, and pervasive unemployment, all conspire to make rural poverty look intractable.

Figure 4-2 Meat processing has become the job of choice for many people in rural areas— including immigrants. Source: Joe Valbuena, U.S. Department of Agriculture

Some analysts, like O'Connor, suggest that poverty is inherent in the structure of capitalism, while others stress the roles of local social capital, entrepreneurial networks, and competition for political office—the latter because political officials help determine the allocation of resources.

The rural poor have another disadvantage: Federal programs and support tend to favor urban places. Metropolitan areas receive two to five times more community development money from the federal government per capita than do rural ones. And what rural areas receive is more likely to take the form of income support programs and subsidies than funding that would encourage greater local community and economic development. Since the advent of the "new federalism" the structural disadvantages faced by rural governments relative to securing federal resources have only become greater.

Food and housing

It is often said of the rural poor that "at least they can grow their own food." But this is a myth. In fact, a growing number of rural counties can be classified as "food deserts," places where individuals have to drive more than 10 miles to the nearest supermarket or major food retailer.

Food insecurity and malnutrition are endemic in rural places. In a case study of Iowa, it was determined that nearly half of rural residents living in a food desert lacked adequate amounts of fresh fruits, about two-thirds lacked adequate amounts of vegetables, a third did not get enough dairy products, and better than a quarter did not get recommended amounts of protein in their diets. In rural food deserts, the problems of the elderly are especially severe given limitations on their transportation options. Of course, food deserts exist in large parts of urban America, as well—giving rural poverty and urban poverty much in common.

While the quality of the housing stock of rural America has seen some real improvement over the last several decades, both housing affordability and access to credit remain problems for rural people. Likewise, the greatest amount of poor quality housing, some still without indoor plumbing, is located in rural areas, especially on Indian reservations and among other minority groups. It is estimated that one in five rural African Americans households lives in substandard housing.

While home ownership rates in rural areas are higher than in urban ones, rural minority groups continue to lag behind. Today the key issue appears to be affordability. This may be one reason why relatively inexpensive manufactured housing remains such a popular housing option. Federal support for low- and moderate-income housing in rural areas has also declined in recent years, making affordability even more difficult. And a long hidden problem, rural homelessness, is only now receiving attention. (See "A Rural Problem, Too," June 2007.)

Greater poverty rates, higher unemployment and underemployment, the prevalence of poor quality housing, and increasing food insecurity all combine to degrade rural public health. Traditionally underserved by health care providers, rural America also tends to be both underinsured and uninsured at higher rates than urban America. In 2003, the U.S. Department of Agriculture estimated that almost 20 percent of all rural people lacked heath insurance.

The burden of poor health care falls most heavily on the elderly and children and is especially acute in rural counties with relatively large Native American populations. Medicaid is available to some, but for rural households with income too high to qualify for Medicaid coverage, there is the federal Children's Health Insurance Program. Between 1998 and

2005, the number of rural low-income children depending on these two programs rose from 38 to 54 percent. The size of the Children's Health Insurance Program, as well as its continuation, was debated in Congress this summer.

These and related problems are longstanding, but new factors have entered the picture as well. The failure to provide rural areas with high-speed Internet and other data and communications infrastructure is a growing barrier to rural development and prosperity. Compared to some other countries, like Canada, the digital divide is much larger in the U.S.

Figure 4-3
Signs of decline: a shuttered motel in Trona, California. Source: Mike Epstein

The lack of transportation alternatives—rural buses, passenger trains, and airline service have been radically reduced over the past several years—also compromises local economic development and the quality of life for countless rural people. And higher energy prices, especially gasoline price increases, pose a burden because rural people have fewer travel options and longer per capita journeys to work than their urban counterparts.

Research likewise indicates that electricity and home heating costs are higher in rural areas than in urban ones. Among farmers, energy—in the form of fertilizers, for example—has traditionally been substituted for labor, and this, too, has become more expensive over the years.

The policy problem

Perhaps unsurprisingly, our rural development policy has been piecemeal or nonexistent. Without doubt, the major U.S. federal law addressing rural needs has been the farm bill. Written about every five years, the law reflects a time now long gone, a time when agriculture and rural life were genuinely synonymous.

In the last several reauthorizations, however, rural development advocates have tried to move the core of the bill, and the vast majority of its funding, away from subsidies and commodity programs to programs that would address various rural problems. This effort has been only minimally successful, in large part because commodity interests remain so entrenched and powerful, even though the numbers they represent are small in comparison to the overall rural population.

The past seven decades have seen major spurts of federal activity to address the problems of persistent rural poverty. Examples include the New Deal, the War on Poverty, and the Great Society. Head Start, Medicaid, Aid to Families with Dependent Children, school lunch and breakfast programs, and numerous other programs have worked at the margins to alleviate rural poverty. In the 1960s, a number of federally supported regional commissions were established to address the overall needs of declining rural regions. Today only the Appalachian Regional Commission remains.

Certain biases have tended to permeate federal rural development efforts. These include a focus on regional instead of local analysis, increased agricultural production as the key mechanism for income growth, a dependence on providing physical infrastructure such as highways and megaprojects like the Tennessee Valley Authority to generate employment, and only a poorly coordinated and sometimes haphazard approach to human capital and community development.

New thinking

New and more creative thinking about rural development has finally begun to emerge. Officials at the Federal Reserve Bank of Kansas City have been focusing on new entrepreneurial networks that emphasize research-intensive commodities and products to meet the needs of emerging niche markets in the global marketplace. They also advocate approaches that stress regional coalitions or collaborations between communities in order to overcome a "beggar thy neighbor" approach to industrial recruiting.

Others, like Charles Fluharty, president of the Rural Policy Research Institute, argue that future federal rural development support ought to provide necessary and appropriate infrastructure, access to broadband and similar resources, community-building capacity, support for local asset-based development, entrepreneurial networks, new approaches to governance through partnerships, relevant research and development activities, and protecting working landscapes. Ultimately, the federal government ought to reestablish a broad social contract with rural America that understands issues of race, gender, immigration, and poverty, he says.

Ranging across nearly all discussions on the future of rural America is the concept of asset-building, whereby rural people create new wealth through small businesses, entrepreneurship and network development, leveraging rural amenities to attract knowledge workers and sponsoring knowledge-based industries with a high value-added potential, a focus on local health and educational investments, and community philanthropy.

In all of this, the role of planners seems crucial. Robust planning systems at all levels must be developed and deployed if real and substantial change in the communities and lives of rural people is to occur. To do otherwise undercuts the very legitimacy of planning and the entire democratic project. Continuing to write off the futures of one-sixth of the nation is, quite simply, not an option.

Mark Lapping is a distinguished professor of planning and public policy at the University of Southern Maine's Edmund S. Muskie School of Public Service. This article was published in October 2007.

Resources

Books. *First Majority-Last Minority: The Transformation of Rural America* by John L. Shover (Northern Illinois University Press, 1976); *Aging in Rural Settings: Life Circumstances and Distinctive Features*, edited by Raymond Coward and J. A. Krout. (Springer, 1998); Alice O'Connor's *Poverty Knowledge: Social Science, Social Policy and the Poor in Twentieth Century America* (Princeton University Press, 2001); *Worlds Apart—Why Poverty Persists in Rural America* by Cynthia M. Duncan (Yale University Press, 1999); Mark B. Lapping's "Rural Policy and Planning" in *Handbook of Rural Studies*, edited by Paul Cloke, Terry Marsden, and Patrick H. Mooney (Sage Publishers, 2006).

Reports and white papers. From the New Carsey Institute of the University of New Hampshire: Kenneth Johnson, *Demographic Trends in Rural and Small Town America*; Kristin Smith and Priscilla Salant, *Rural America Depends on the Food Stamp Program to Make Ends Meet*; Kristin Smith and Sarah Savage, *Food Stamp and School Lunch Programs Alleviate Food Insecurity in Rural America*.

From the Federal Reserve Bank of Kansas City: "New Federalism—Problems in Opportunities for Rural America" by Sara

A. Low in *The Main Street Economist: Commentary on the Rural Economy*, 2005. "Reinventing the Rural Economy" by Mark Drabenstott, in *The Main Street Economist*, December 2004. Other federal sources: *Rural America at a Glance: 2006*, Economic Research Service, U.S. Department of Agriculture, August 2006. Charles W. Fluharty, "Leading the Rural Renaissance," USDA Rural Development Policy Meeting, Dallas, January 9, 2007.

From nonprofits: National Rural Network's *Why Rural Matters III: The Rural Impact of the Administration's FY08 Budget Proposal*. Housing Assistance Council, *Taking Stock: Rural People, Poverty, and Housing at the Turn of the 21st Century*, 2002. From the Rural Sociology Society: *The Challenges of Rural Poverty*, 2006, and Lois Wright Morton and Troy C. Blanchard's *Starved for Access: Life in Rural America's Food Deserts*, 2007.

Also: *The Causes of Enduring Poverty: An Expanded Spatial Analysis of the Structural Determinants of Poverty in the U.S.* by Anil Rupasingha and Stephan J. Goetz, Northeast Regional Center for Rural Development, Pennsylvania State University, 2003.

Periodicals. From *Planning*: Mark B. Lapping's "Viewpoint," May 2007. Paul Rollinson, "A Rural Problem Too: Homelessness Beyond the Big Cities," June 2007.

Newspaper articles: Richard Mertens, "In Rural America, Community Philanthropy Thrives," *Christian Science Monitor*, May 24, 2007. Doug Rauthe, "Rural Kids Lack Health Insurance," *The Helena (Mont.) Independent Record*, May 28, 2007.

Journal articles: "Small Town Philanthropy," by Suzanne Perry, in *The Chronicle of Philanthrophy*, July 26, 2007. "Entrepreneurial Social Infrastructures and Locally Initiated Economic Development in the Nonmetropolitan United States," by J. L. Flora, J. Sharp, C. B. Flora, and B. Newton, in *The Sociological Quarterly*, 1997. Patricia McGrath Morris, Linda Neuhauser, and Cathy Campbell wrote "Food Security in Rural America: A Study of the Availability and Costs of Food," in *Journal of Nutrition Education*, 1992.

ENVIRONMENTAL (IN)JUSTICE
Have we made any progress in the last 25 years?
By James Krohe Jr.

"It was a death sentence," Sheila Holt-Orsted told the press in May of last year, when describing the plague of cancers that she and her family have suffered in recent years. She thinks the culprit is a well that was poisoned with the industrial solvent trichloroethylene, or TCE.

Holt-Orsted knows who was responsible for the pollution: local officials who in 1968 put a landfill barely 50 feet from her property in an unincorporated, rural black hamlet in Dickson County, Tennessee. And she suspects the reason why: because she and her family are African American. Her white neighbors across the city line were drawing from the same polluted groundwater but were hooked up to a safe municipal supply years before she was.

The poisoning of the Holts' well, and the clumsy official response to it, point to an unpleasant truth: Your health depends on where you live. In the U.S., toxic waste dumps and polluting industries are sited disproportionately in communities whose residents are poor or people of color.

"The Dickson case is the current poster child of the environmental justice movement in the U.S.," says Robert Bullard, director of the Environmental Justice Resource Center at Clark Atlanta University. "It's the best example of 'racialized' place and government-sanctioned planning and decision making [that places] African Americans at special risk. When this landfill was put there in 1968, black people had very little representation. Blacks only make up about four percent of the county population, but all of the landfills in the county were sited in [the same] area, which had been all-black for five generations."

Stories like that of the Holts abound. Many illnesses—among them cancers, thyroid disorders, and breathing difficulties—have been attributed to the proximity of locally unwanted land uses, or LULUs. In El Paso and nearby towns it is a copper smelter. In Mossville, an African American hamlet on the outskirts of Lake Charles, Louisiana, it is air pollution from vinyl manufacturing plants. In Ford Heights, outside Chicago, it's a tire incinerator. In south Seattle it is idling trucks at a freight terminal. In Commerce, California, it is intermodal rail yards. In San Antonio it is the industrial redevelopment of a former Air Force base.

No one has definitively proven that the many ills reported by the neighbors of these facilities were caused by environmental exposure, because the state of science makes that determination impossible. But while the actual harm from such sources may be disputed, there is no disputing that the risk of harm from polluting industries, past and present, is being borne disproportionately by the nation's marginalized populations.

Environmental racism?

The environmental justice movement as such is usually reckoned to have begun in Houston, where city officials in 1979 were blocked by a lawsuit from siting a toxic waste site in an urban black neighborhood. Not long after that, local protests about the siting of a state polychlorinated biphenyl (PCB) landfill in the mostly black Afton community in Warren County, North Carolina, attracted national attention.

Warren County awakened many an activist to environmental discrimination. One of those was Clark Atlanta's Robert Bullard, who would become a leading voice on environmental justice matters. "The county put that in knowing it would leak," he says today. "We're not talking about something that happened during slavery—that happened 21 years ago."

Among the Warren County protestors was District of Columbia Delegate Walter E. Fauntroy. Sensing that Warren County was not an isolated incident, Fauntroy asked the U.S. General Accounting Office to study the siting of hazardous waste landfills in the eight states of the Deep South. The GAO study found that three of the region's four off-site hazardous-waste landfills were located in communities that were majority African American.

In 1987, the United Church of Christ commissioned what became a landmark study, "Toxic Wastes and Race in the United States," that examined five variables related to the siting of hazardous waste sites. The study found that the surest predictor was the race of the people who lived nearby. African Americans were most likely to live near such sites. Hispanics and Asians were less likely to, but still much more so than whites.

That finding has been confirmed by many subsequent studies, including a widely cited 2005 study of Environmental Protection Agency data that was conducted by the Associated Press. It found that African Americans were 79 percent more likely than white Americans to live in a neighborhood where industrial pollution is suspected of posing health risks. In 12 states Hispanics are more than twice as likely as non-Hispanics to live in neighborhoods with the highest risks to health from pollution, and in seven states it is Asians who are much more likely than whites to live in such areas.

According to one study, these disparities are getting worse. The United Church of Christ recently commissioned four university scholars to update the 1987 study. The authors examined 413 facilities nationwide that process or store hazardous chemical waste. In 2007, as documented in the report "Toxic Wastes and Race at Twenty," African Americans and other people of color are more likely to live near currently operating commercial hazardous waste facilities today than they were two decades ago.

People of color now make up 56 percent of the residents living in neighborhoods within two miles of these facilities. The state where the highest percentage of such residents are minorities—81 percent—is California, a state that is both highly industrialized and substantially nonwhite. In greater Los Angeles it was even worse: 91 percent of the 1.2 million people living less than two miles from such facilities were minorities.

That study also found that nearly seven in 10 of the residents in neighborhoods with clusters of waste facilities are people of color. "Other research has found that new sitings in recent decades have been increasingly directed toward the urban core," says Robin Saha, assistant professor of environmental studies at University of Montana and coauthor of the United Church of Christ report.

Figure 4-4
Sheila Holt-Orsted grieving at her father's grave in Tennessee. She believes family illnesses can be traced to toxins in the family well. Source: © The Washington Post Writers Group, photo by Carol Guzy. Reprinted with permission.

In the inner cities, new noxious facilities are opening in areas already burdened with industrial pollution. One example is the Little Village-Pilsen area of Chicago, home to the largest Mexican American population in the U.S. outside of East Los Angeles. It is also home to the only two coal-burning power plants left within 40 miles of downtown Chicago, a waste transfer station, and the city's largest steel drum recycling plant and its largest plastic recycler. Also, four of the city's 10 dirtiest diesel truck corridors pass through Little Village. As a result, the air in the neighborhood is so dirty that public health officials estimate it causes 41 premature deaths, 2,800 asthma attacks, and 550 emergency room visits every year.

"Emissions are not the only threat," adds Saha. "Communities are shouldered with the burden of truck traffic with its noise and fumes, and the risk of explosions, accidents, and spills."

A national problem

While most of the early controversies over the siting of noxious land uses occurred in the South, "we found disparities in nine of 10 regions of the country," says Robert Bullard in describing the "Toxic Wastes and Race at Twenty" report. "That's a national problem." The Associated Press analysis of U.S. EPA data found that among the 19 states in which blacks were more than twice as likely as whites to live in neighborhoods where air pollution risk ranked highest were Missouri, Kansas, Kentucky, Minnesota, Oregon, and Wisconsin.

Many activists insist that corporations seek out places whose residents may be politically impotent, or so badly in need of jobs that they will accept risks that better fixed communities would not. The strategy has the effect of targeting people of color, activists add, since political disengagement and poverty are related.

This tends to be true of any marginalized peoples, including white ones. Long before attention was drawn to the plight of blacks, the nation was aware of the poisoned creeks, landslides, and other hazards associated with coal mining in the mountains of Kentucky and West Virginia. The Sierra Club maintains a Central Appalachia Environmental Justice site to support the work of activists trying to counter what the organization calls "the irresponsible practices of the mining industry."

Further, the two counties where new hazardous or radioactive waste landfills were successfully sited in the late 1980s—Adams County, Colorado, and Tooele County, Utah—were at the time 87 percent and 92 percent white, respectively.

The stories beneath the headlines

News accounts of environmental justice tend to reduce complex health-related pollution stories to simple heroes-and-villains tales. The facts very often tell a more complex story. In the 1990s, the San Bernardino County city of Redlands—then mostly white, and mostly middle-class—learned that its groundwater was contaminated by the industrial chemical perchlorate from the plant of the aerospace giant Lockheed Martin. Within a year, the Santa Ana Regional Water Quality Control Board issued a strong cleanup and abatement order that obliged Lockheed Martin to spend millions on water purification systems capable of removing perchlorate from local drinking water wells.

A few miles away is the working class town of Rialto, a freight transshipment center whose population was then about 70 percent Latino and one-fifth African American. Perchlorate was contaminating the groundwater there, too. However, to date the Regional Water Board has yet to adopt a strong final cleanup order against the corporate polluters most responsible for the poisoned groundwater in Rialto, mainly because of what critics call the companies' stalling tactics.

"The regional water board has not done its job from day one," says Jan Misquez of the San Bernadino office of the Center for Community Action and Environmental Justice. "The plume moves two feet a day and it's eating hundreds of thousands of gallons of clean water every day." Meanwhile the taxpayers of Rialto must pay to treat their water through a water bill surcharge.

Why did the two towns receive disparate treatment? As it happens, plain old-fashioned political favoritism may have been a factor. One of the members of the Santa Ana Regional Water Quality Control Board that acted so promptly in the case of Redlands was a resident and former mayor of Redlands. And in Redlands, liability for the pollution was clear, but in Rialto, 42 parties were legally responsible for a cleanup.

The story of the Holts' TCE-poisoned well in Dickson County, Tennessee, was also complicated. The Holts say they were officially assured their water was safe in 1988 and 1991, although further tests persuaded local authorities to connect them to the municipal supply in 2000. According to a federal civil rights claim filed by the family in 2004, their white neighbors were warned of toxins in their private wells and were hooked up to city water as far back as 1993.

That looked like racism to the media. This was a typical headline: "A Well of Pain: Their Water Was Poisoned by Chemicals. Was Their Treatment Poisoned by Racism?"

However, the events could be interpreted as the results of official ineptitude and bureaucratic self-protection. By 1988, the county had been cited for violations of state groundwater regulations more than once, but years later, when a test in 2000 did show unambiguously dangerous levels of TCE, local authorities acted immediately to take the Holts off well water.

By then the dithering had gone on for years, during which time the Holts continued to use the well. Asked why the Holt well was not tested sooner, the general counsel for the state's Department of Environment and Conservation said the state's resources were focused on the places where TCE levels were even higher than at the Holts' and that property owners who choose to rely on private wells instead of municipal water are responsible for monitoring the wells' safety—something the Holt didn't do because, they say, they didn't know they were supposed to.

Who's responsible?

Industry, governments at all levels, and planners have all added environmental justice to their agendas. They bring varying degrees of commitment, resources, and urgency to the problem.

"Leadership must come from the top," says Bullard. "Even though land-use planning is local, there should be federal guidances that inform local decisions so you're not getting states using different criteria to address and redress past siting inequities. That is not to say that the feds should step into local planning and development, but they have an oversight role to play."

Under the administrations of George H.W. Bush and Bill Clinton, environmental justice was put on the crowded federal agenda when the U.S. EPA set up administrative machinery to study the issue. The EPA can classify as an "Environmental Justice Community of Concern" a neighborhood or community composed of predominantly poor or minority residents that it regards as "environmentally overburdened" and impose stricter-than-usual emissions or monitoring standards on facilities operating within it.

In 1993 a collection of 12 federal agencies called the Interagency Working Group of Environmental Justice was set up to integrate environmental justice into the individual programs of 11 federal agencies, with leadership from EPA.

By far the most significant federal action in those years was President Clinton's 1994 Executive Order 12898. It directed all federal agencies to make environmental justice part of their missions by ensuring that policies and operations were consistent with Title VI of the Civil Rights Act of 1964, which bans discrimination in government-funded programs and projects, and the National Environmental Policy Act of 1969, which requires the assessment of environmental impacts as part of major project reviews.

The Clinton order has not been embraced by the second President Bush, whose administration has rejected on principle policies that single out any one race or income group. (The Clinton executive order does not have the force of law, and Congress has not acted to make it law.) The EPA's inspector general has found that, 14 years after the order was signed, the EPA "cannot determine whether its programs cause disproportionately high and adverse human health or environmental effects on communities of color and low-income populations."

EPA's Title VI regulations allow citizens to file administrative complaints that allege discrimination by EPA-funded programs. (That includes the state EPAs that issue the operating permits for polluting facilities.) Those environmental justice reviews, says environmental attorney Michael Gerrard, have proven "utterly ineffective."

States step up

The U.S. EPA sets many basic environmental standards, but the states have the primary responsibility for enforcing them. In recent years, the Public Law Research Institute of Hastings College of the Law at the University of California has compiled an annual report entitled *Environmental Justice for All: A Fifty State Survey of Legislation, Policies and Cases*. At least 32 states and the District of Columbia have adopted formal environmental justice statutes, executive orders, or policies. (The pioneer was New Hampshire, which adopted its environmental justice policy in 1993.) Of those 32 states, 10 either employ full-time environmental justice officers or personnel, or have active environmental justice programs.

Minorities remain underrepresented on most of the boards and commissions that site and regulate polluting industries, including zoning boards. Responding to that gap, the states are expanding opportunities for public participation. New Mexico held a statewide series of "listening sessions" in 2004. Delaware and New Jersey are among the states to create standing environmental justice advisory boards (with required community representation), which can serve as clearinghouses for information and lines of communication among stakeholder groups.

California is one of the states that has taken a comprehensive approach to environmental justice, complete with strategy documents, action plans, and interagency agreements. Since 1997, California's Air Quality Management Districts have had an environmental justice program "to ensure that everyone has the right to equal protection from air pollution and fair access to the decision-making process. . . . regardless of race, age, culture, income, or geographic location."

In many phases of pollution abatement, local governments are mere observers. They do have a major role to play, however, in deciding where to put any of the ever-widening range of facilities that pose health risks to their human neighbors. In short, it is often local officials who decide—in Bullard's words—"who gets the goods, and who get the bads."

Metropolitan planning organizations, which are federally funded, have been obliged to meet the Federal Highway Administration's environmental justice procedures since 1994. However, some question whether that practice has been done in a systematic, proactive way. "MPOs are dealing with waste management, air quality, solid waste disposal—all are environmental justice issues," notes Bullard, "yet very few plans use an environmental justice framework to show how public investments are being made."

In 2001 the Delaware Valley Regional Planning Commission unveiled its "And Justice for All" strategy for fair treatment and meaningful involvement of all people. Using GIS, the agency applies a "degrees of disadvantage" overlay of six indicators—minority, Hispanic, low-income, elderly, transportation-dependent, and handicapped populations—to gauge the impact of its transportation plans.

A few MPOs have had to be nudged. For years, the Wisconsin ACLU has raised questions about the poor quality of the low-income and minority impact analysis done by the Southeastern Wisconsin Regional Planning Commission, which serves the seven-county Milwaukee metro area. The ACLU has alleged that the commission's highway planning is racially biased because nearly one-third of all African Americans in Milwaukee do not even have driver's licenses.

Responding to that criticism, the commission recently established a 15-member task force on environmental justice, an advisory body meant to provide another, presumably broader avenue for public participation during the planning process. "What we're trying to do is put together a regional plan while paying regard to very local impacts," says Ken Yunker, the commission's deputy director.

How local is local enough?

For decades, planners have pressed local officials to take a regional approach to the environment. Now planners can find themselves damned for bringing a perspective to industrial siting decisions that is not local enough.

Consider the issue of mitigation. Cleaning up or shutting down polluting facilities can be expensive or economically unfeasible, as is relocating them or the people living near them. Where feasible, polluters can be made to pay to reduce pollution from other sources nearby in the hope of reducing, or at least not increasing, the health risk carried by residents.

California's South Coast Air Quality Management District, which takes in most of Los Angeles and adjacent counties, last summer began considering the permit request for a new power plant in the city of Vernon. One proposal would require Vernon to pay nearly $50 million in mitigation fees, including roughly $50,000 per pound for emissions of PM10—the tiny soot particles that, along with coarser dust, are estimated to contribute to 5,400 premature deaths and 2,400 hospitalizations in the region each year. Such fees would be paid in lieu of the strictest control measures, and are used to fund control measures elsewhere in the airshed.

"The problem with mitigation is that it usually doesn't happen in the affected community," says Angelo Logan, executive director of East Yard

Communities for Environmental Justice, based in nearby Commerce. "Say you have a power plant emitting PM10 that pays the fees, and those funds go to put a control device on a chrome plating plant that's also emitting PM10. If I live 1.5 miles from the power plant and five miles from the other device, that doesn't do me much good. That's more a macro than a micro approach. It may work regionally but doesn't address environmental justice concerns in particular communities."

When agencies fail

The courts provided justice to aggrieved African Americans during the early days of the civil rights movement, when legislatures were unresponsive. Litigants claiming to be victims of environmental injustice have not seen the same results.

Residents living near a pollution source can sue for damages under common law, but specific damages from diffuse pollution usually is hard to prove. Further, environmental law does not generally authorize compensation for lost property value, and most states ban compensation to private parties, if they permit compensation at all.

State courts can be more receptive than federal courts to environmental justice claims. Some are willing to determine whether socioeconomic effects and quality of life should be considered in official decisions. In California, private citizens have the right to sue state agencies for decisions that have discriminatory effects, including siting of facilities and the composition of planning or advisory boards.

If the bureaucracies and the courts fail, conventional pressure group politics can sometimes offer means of redress. When residents of Rialto grew frustrated at the slow pace at which the Santa Ana Regional Water Quality Control Board was cleaning up the perchlorate that contaminated their drinking water, a coalition of state and local green groups in the summer of 2006 (in their words) "pulled out all the stops" with a media campaign to focus public attention to the problem.

Several members of the regional board who were up for confirmation, including the chair, were called to the state capital by the state senate to publicly testify about why it was taking so long. The water board thereafter promised to speed things up and issued a draft cleanup order that included the criteria developed by the community.

Companies can play politics, too, often by undertaking good neighbor projects. These are intended to persuade or at least to defuse the distrust that so often makes relations between company and nearby residents anything but neighborly.

Amid its ongoing effort to gain community support for its controversial offshore natural gas terminal, Broadwater Energy, whose parent is Shell Oil, in 2007 announced a 10-year, $10 million initiative to fund the weatherizing of more than 2,000 houses in low-income parts of Nassau and Suffolk counties in New York State.

Among the backers of the program are the local National Association for the Advancement of Colored People and the Association of Community Organizations for Reform Now, or ACORN, a community organization of low- and moderate-income families that would administer the program. ACORN's executive director, Bertha Lewis, told a local reporter, "Usually when people build energy facilities, they put them in our neighborhoods. We think this makes sense nine miles offshore."

That was not the opinion of opponents of the offshore gas terminal, who dismissed the weatherization program as "a successful cooptation of the activist group ACORN" and "'a bribe to bring good public relations points."

25 years later

The environmental justice movement is now a quarter-century old. In that time, everything and nothing about the issues have changed. From the original focus on African Americans, the roster of affected people has expanded to include Native Americans, indigenous peoples of the Artic, immigrants and refugees, the disabled, and uneducated communities.

Originally, the targets of ire were leaking waste dumps or dirty incinerators. Today they stretch across a range of noxious facilities. And justice is now considered an aspect not only of siting or cleanup but program design, standard setting, permitting, enforcement, and brownfield redevelopment, even the racial composition of mainstream environmental groups' leadership and staff.

Similarly, "environment" is being enlarged to take in more than pollution-caused illness. The Clinton Executive Order of 1994 listed 11 adverse effects to be avoided, of which only two were contamination and health impairments. Today, "environmental justice is much more than toxics and wastes and siting of noxious facilities and LULUs," says Robert Bullard. "It is also about land use, healthy and sustainable communities, equitable development, sprawl and smart growth, regional equity, transportation, energy, clean production, green jobs, climate change, etc. All have implications for planning and planners."

An example of transportation-related equity is a policy adopted by AASHTO, the American Association of State Highway and Transportation Officials. That organization directs the attention of its members to the exclusionary effects on the poor of roadbuilders' dependence on toll revenue to fund and maintain new and existing roadways.

As the movement achieves more, it hopes for more. The more extreme advocates insist that poor minorities should not endure higher levels of health risk than affluent people do. The cure, therefore, is not a more open process, or more thorough environmental vetting of sites, or more rigorous land-use planning. In this view, the solution is for no one to live within three miles of any polluting site. A noble ideal—but one that would require shutting down U.S. cities.

Justice and injustice
Reducing the problem of hazardous waste sites would require cleaning up thousands of old factory properties—for which there is not remotely enough money—or relocating millions of Americans. Of course, the reason so many poor and minorities end up near noxious LULUs in the first place—leaving aside for the moment the possibility that such land uses are being deliberately installed next door—is because housing there is cheap. Giving residents of such places a choice means generally giving the poor more housing and transportation options—themselves massive undertakings.

If, as Bullard says, economic justice is the ultimate cure for environmental injustice, we'll have a long wait. Christopher Foreman, who directs the social policy program at the University of Maryland School of Public Policy, testified in 2002 before the U.S. Commission on Civil Rights. "We should try harder than we do to address the most egregious imbalances and risks that result [from siting disparities]. But we are not going to abolish the market economy or private property," he said at the time.

Still, steps can be taken to right some wrongs. Michael Gerrard has offered several real-world solutions, including holding referenda on siting in which the entire local electorate decides rather than the community's governing body. Another suggestion is to award compensation that allows a site's closest neighbors to move out if they wish. The most recent United Church of Christ report also contains a number of policy recommendations, including requiring nonresidential buffer zones around new noxious facilities.

And about what is being done? On the release of the updated United Church of Christ report, coauthor Paul Mohai, professor of environmental justice at the University of Michigan School of Natural Resources and Environment, said the results to date are dismaying. "You can see there has been a lot more attention to the issue of environmental justice but the progress has been very, very slow," Mohai said. "Why? As important as all those efforts are, they haven't been well executed and I don't know if the political will is there."

Indeed, some argue that the problem is not that too little is being done about environmental justice, but that too much might be done. The California Council for Environmental and Economic Balance, which calls itself that state's only private, nonprofit, nonpartisan association to represent the interests of both industry and labor, warns that "environmental justice policy can help identify and correct public health problems, but should neither be expected nor required to resolve broader issues of social injustice or past ill-advised land-use planning and urban design."

The *Chicago Tribune* made the same point editorially in 1998. "Ultimately the way to ensure that minorities are not disproportionately affected by environmental risks is to concentrate on the science and skip the politics: Industrial installations should meet environmental standards no matter where they are located. And those that don't shouldn't be allowed to operate anywhere in the first place."

Christopher Foreman, among others, argues that a focus on environmental justice risks aggravating economic inefficiency and paralyzing local planning. It also risks diverting community attention from more serious environmental risks and problems. (As *The Economist* put it in a recent editorial, the lead in bullets is a more immediate health risk than leaking landfills in many minority neighborhoods.)

Planning in an environmental justice context is often a matter of making the least wrong choice among those that are possible. Because of the environmental justice movement, the civil rights movement began to think green, and the green movement began to embrace social justice as a goal, arguably to the improvement of both.

And sometimes old injustices are remedied. In 2004, after more than two decades, state and federal agencies finished detoxifying 81,500 tons of the contaminated soil stored at the PCB landfill in Warren County, North Carolina, whose plight in many ways triggered the start of the environmental justice movement in 1982. And while new hazardous waste sites may be more concentrated in vulnerable neighborhoods than they were 25 years ago, there are many fewer of them—thanks in part, says Robin Saha, to "the resistance that communities of color are putting up."

James Krohe Jr. is a Chicago-based writer. This article was published in March 2008.

The Science

Regulators, business groups, and mainstream environmentalists agree that pollution control regulations and the environmental justice policies based on them should be rooted in good science. But when it comes to environmental justice, even the science is politicized.

The public meeting is the forum in which many of the conflicts get voiced. But often participants can't even agree on the issues to address. Jim Throgmorton, a University of Iowa professor of urban and regional planning, tells his students that how one sees the issue of environmental justice depends on where one is standing: "A minority community that's exposed to toxic chemicals would talk about it in terms of justice, whereas a scientist would talk about it in terms of, for example, measurable risk."

Parents expose their children to risk all the time, from secondhand smoke to too many sweets. But they turn protective when someone else puts their kids at risk. The city of Chicago wants to turn a Superfund site in the Little Village neighborhood into a park for kids. The corporate owner of the site is willing to bury the wastes under three feet of new clean dirt trucked in for the purpose. But the parents are demanding that the contaminated soil be completely removed and replaced, a demand that has left the site fenced and unused for years.

The U.S. EPA describes its mission in part as ensuring that "all people are protected from significant risks to human health and the environment where they live, learn and work." "Significant" is the debatable term. What is not significant to the body of a grown man may be highly significant to an infant or the elderly.

In 2005, scientists of the public interest Institute for Energy and Environmental Research reminded the EPA administrator that the agency calculates radiation health risks for the general population using a hypothetical "Reference Man" or "Standard Man" that is defined as being 20 to 30 years of age, weighing about 155 pounds, measuring five feet seven inches, Caucasian and of Western European or North American heritage.

They added their opinion that public health and environmental protection should offer systematic protection of those most at risk of health problems from exposure to radiation and toxic chemicals: "Unless the EPA actually makes an effort to determine how different communities and groups are affected by toxic chemicals and radiation, it cannot have a basis for creating a policy that is fair."

Resources

In print. *Garbage Wars: The Struggle for Environmental Justice in Chicago*, David Naguib Pellow. *Race and the Incidence of Environmental Hazards: A Time for Discourse*, Bunyan Bryant and Paul Mohai, 1992. *Noxious New York: The Racial Politics of Urban Health* *and Environmental Justice,* Julie Sze, 2006. *Power, Justice, and the Environment: A Critical Appraisal of the Environmental Justice Movement,* David Naguib Pellow and Robert J. Brulle, 2005. *The Promise and Peril of Environmental Justice,* Christopher Foreman, 1998. "Toxic Wastes and Race in the United States: A National Report on the Racial and Socio-economic Characteristics of Communities with Hazardous Waste Sites," United Church of Christ Commission for Racial Justice, 1987. "Toxic Wastes and Race at Twenty, 1987-2007. Grassroots Struggles to Dismantle Environmental Racism in the United States," United Church of Christ Commission for Racial Justice, 2007. "Environmental Justice for All: A 50-State Survey of Legislation, Policy, and Initiatives," Public Law Research Institute of Hastings College of the Law, University of California. *Deeper Shades of Green,* by APA senior researcher Jim Schwab, AICP, was published in 1994.

Organizations and projects. United Church of Christ Commission for Racial Justice: www.ucc.org. Public Law Research Institute, Hastings College of Law: www.uchastings. edu/?pid=134. Sierra Club Environment Justice Projects: www. sierraclub.org. Environmental Justice Database, Michigan State University: www.msu.edu. Environmental Justice Resource Center, Clark Atlanta University: www.ejrc.cau.edu. Center for Community Action and Environmental Justice: www. chej.org.

Government agencies. U.S. EPA: www.epa.gov. U.S. Department of Housing and Urban Development: www.hud.gov. Federal Highway Administration: www.fhwa.dot.gov.

POOR RELATIONS

Suburbs that struggle

By David Peterson

The suburb of Richfield, on the southern edge of Minneapolis, is a seven-square-mile, shoebox-shaped community surrounded by success. After wobbling, even staggering, through the 1980s and early 1990s, Minneapolis is springing back: A $500 million arts building boom is but one sign of the rebound. To the west of Richfield is Edina, home of a handsome share of the region's elites, including the billionaire owner of the Minnesota Twins. To its south lies the mighty Mall of America.

Then there's Richfield itself: the poor relation

Richfield (pop. 34,400) is a typical postwar suburb, its rows of gridded streets lined with look-alike bungalows. It was never wealthy; decades ago, seniors at Edina High School wickedly proposed as a homecoming slogan, not the customary "Tame the Tigers" but rather "Buy Richfield." But, as recently as the late 1970s, Richfield still felt like a traditional suburb in the best sense: quiet, leafy, and orderly, though getting on in years.

Bruce Palmborg, Richfield's engagingly self-deprecating director of planning, recalls 1990 as the low point. "Things weren't looking too good for us," he says. Richfield had awakened to a chilling truth: The market was passing it by. Middle-class families were no longer interested in its 1,100-square-foot houses. And those who might have been were being guided away from the town. Ethnically, racially, and financially, Richfield's character was changing rapidly.

In the mid-1990s, the city began battling back, becoming, among other things, the state's poster child for a free-swinging use of eminent domain. Richfield condemned scores of properties as "blighted" to make way for the new corporate headquarters for Best Buy, replacing auto dealers along a major freeway with a stylish new campus.

Still, a number of Richfield's vital signs continue to flag. On a University of Minnesota website, a series of maps and pie charts show how Richfield has changed year by year. The public schools' numbers of low-income students have grown annually, until most look more like inner city schools than suburban ones. Earlier this year, a drug kingpin was caught while living in the city, in what a reporter referred to as a "rented matchbox house in Richfield."

What the numbers mean

None of this surprises Robert Puentes, a fellow in metropolitan policy at the Brookings Institution who has studied what he calls the nation's "first suburbs." He is accustomed to seeing what he calls "a neat ring of distress, right around the central city." And he pays particular attention to the trajectory of growth in poverty. "When you reach poverty concentrations of 20 percent, 30 percent, 40 percent, schools start failing, crime becomes rampant, and it becomes very difficult to pull out of that," he says.

Earlier this year, William Lucy, AICP, and David Phillips, AICP, professors of urban planning at the University of Virginia, looked at inner cities and their close-in suburbs in a new way. For a book called *Tomorrow's Cities, Tomorrow's Suburbs* (published in January by APA's Planners Press), they created a list of communities in 35 major metropolitan areas that—on paper at least—are worse off than Detroit. They picked Detroit as the basis of comparison because, in terms of per capita income relative to its metro area, it scores lower than all other big cities. To be worse off than Detroit means a per capita income of less than 60 percent of the metro area as a whole.

Using figures from the 2000 census and excluding cities with populations smaller than 2,000, the researchers found 155 in worse shape than Detroit—about 50 of them had dropped to that point during the 1990s. The list raises—without setting out to answer—some interesting questions: Where are these suburbs? What happened? And, as the mayor of one of them put it, "How do I get off this list?"

Although the list aims to dramatize the vulnerabilities of suburbs, some of the listed cities aren't really suburban. They are cities located in metropolitan counties, but far enough from the central city to be considered poor and rural rather than poor and metropolitan.

Some make the list for quirky reasons; a few are college towns, where students drag down the averages. College Park, the home of the University of Maryland, makes the list, as does Prairie View, Texas. In that city, home to Prairie View A&M, 70 percent of the 4,658 residents are between the ages of 18 and 24.

Other suburbs are ancient by American standards, as old as or older than the bigger cities nearby. Chelsea, a Boston suburb, is one of them; so is Chester, near Philadelphia. Chester's present-day struggles are nothing new, says a website devoted to the city's history. It reprints a comment published in an 1817 newspaper article: "Chester was formerly a place of considerable commerce; but at present, of very little. The warehouses, and buildings nearest the water, are generally in a neglected and decaying state; presenting a melancholy picture of the 'gleams of better days.'"

Many of the struggling communities are small, both in surface area and population. St. Louis, in particular, is edged by a jumble of microsuburbs whose sheer minuteness is probably part of what makes them vulnerable, says Puentes, who adds that that dynamic of fragmentation is now a focus of research at Brookings.

The forces that created today's Richfield—matchbox houses, cheaply built apartment buildings without elevators or air conditioning, the remorseless momentum that sets in as poorer people arrive—are plainly at work in many of the 155 communities singled out by Bill Lucy and David Phillips. After the 1990 census, the *Los Angeles Times* listed a group of area suburbs in which at least eight of every 10 residents were Hispanic: Huntington Park, Bell, Bell Gardens, Commerce, Cudahy, Maywood, Pico Rivera, South Gate. All are on the list of 155, and all but one made it by 1990.

"Let me put it this way," the city manager of Maywood told the newspaper after the 1990 census was released. "I have lived on my block for 28 years. It used to be all Anglo. Today, there are four or five Anglos left." He was commenting on an ethnic change that clearly corresponded to a statistical decline in affluence, particularly when figured on a per capita basis.

News coverage of these kinds of communities is the same everywhere. To read a number of headlines in succession is to see a blur of sameness: "Gang killing" and "Fiscal crisis in inner ring as state mulls takeover of low-performing schools."

Change and pain

There's a vivid portrayal of what has happened to some of these places on a website in Hamtramck, Michigan, an old Polish-American industrial enclave surrounded entirely by the city of Detroit. Hamtramck (pop. 23,000) has lived through wrenching times, as long-term residents have watched a new wave of Muslim immigrants arrive—a discomfort dramatized by a fight over the new arrivals' desire to broadcast calls to prayer over public loudspeakers.

"That was definitely threatening to some people here, even frightening," says Karen Majewski, the city's mayor. "When new people come in, it doesn't matter who they are; it's always an uncomfortable mix."

The website is comprised in large part of a series of pitiless photos of what the city has become: In one image, homes with barely a lick of paint left stand beside empty lots overgrown with weeds. In another, a crude handpainted sign—"MURFF'S MKT BEER WINE"—sticks out from a shack with bars on the windows.

"We're a prototypical old Rust Belt city with aging infrastructure that is beyond our means to repair," Majewski says. "Some of our sewers are still made of wood. We were placed in emergency financial status in 2000 and it hasn't been lifted yet, though we expect that to happen this year and we are back in the black."

East St. Louis makes the professors' list of distressed suburbs. So does East Palo Alto, California, where, according to Stanford's student newspaper, students go to buy their drugs. East Los Angeles makes it, as does East Cleveland, Ohio, with its Wall of Sorrows, the facade of a decaying building where hundreds of names of victims of violence have been posted over the years.

Chasing a tax base

It is striking to see, on a virtual tour of the poor relations, an enthusiasm for attracting developments that richer places fight off.

Big-box retail proposals in the Twin Cities area often start big fights (a planning commission member in tony Edina recently declared that no parcel in the city is suitable for such a store), but Richfield is becoming a big-box haven, even invoking eminent domain to clear small businesses and make room for more.

Wal-Mart is finding a ready home in many of these places. "We had a Wal-Mart go in a couple of years ago, with no controversy, or very little," says Roger Post, AICP, planning director in National City, California (pop. 54,300), a suburb of San Diego. "We're working with Costco right now, trying get them into town. We're real focused on economic sustainability, and that's a part of that," he says.

Casinos, too, have landed in some of these suburbs. Near Philadelphia, the town of Chester (pop. 36,900) is delighted to have seen over $1 billion in development in the past decade, the largest piece of which is Harrah's Chester Casino & Racetrack, a harness racing track with 2,500 slot machines. The casino portion is set to open by early next year.

"We don't have much tax base, and that's a big issue," says Adriene Irving, the city's director of communications. "Our housing stock is old, and we have such a large number of families below poverty. They're renting, lots of them through Section 8, which causes problems. We recently built a small housing development that represents our first new single-family homes in 30 years or so."

"We have all kinds of incentives to attract businesses," she adds. "But it continues to be a struggle. It will take a little while. We didn't get to this point overnight."

There are success stories. Commerce City, Colorado, located between Denver and the Denver International Airport, is the site of a stadium for the local Major League Soccer team that will also serve as an outdoor concert venue when it opens in 2007. This is the kind of use that wealthier suburbs often battle each other to get. It's a triumph in a community that started the decade with worse-than-Detroit income numbers, a population that was 40 percent renters, and only four percent with college degrees.

"We're very excited about it," says Heather Grady, the city's spokeswoman.

Commerce City has one thing going for it that many other struggling suburbs do not: open, developable land. Because there is room to build, the community's population grew from 16,000 in 1990 to an estimated 34,000 in 2005. Building permits shot from fewer than 200 in 2000 to more than 1,500 last year. "Our location," Grady says, "is our prime asset."

Figure 4-5
Richfield, Minnesota, a postwar suburb of Minneapolis, has been battling decline with such tools as eminent domain. Source: David Peterson

Use your assets

There was a time when being close to downtown didn't seem like much of an asset. But in these days of highway congestion and accelerating downtown revival, inner-ring suburbs are eager to trumpet how few minutes of travel divide them and the sparkling new amenities of the central city.

Riverdale, Illinois, about 20 miles south of downtown Chicago, has been in economic freefall in recent decades. Now it is touting its proximity to downtown. A video on the city's website, called "Things to Do," turns out to have not so much Riverdale itself in mind: It begins by mentioning "all the advantages of living on the border of Chicago, a city with world-renowned shopping, dining, museums, architecture, theater, sports, and music."

Likewise, one of the first things Roger Post brings up about National City is its location just five minutes from downtown San Diego. "You can buy a house in Riverside County and drive an hour and a half to get there, but you don't have much of your life left," he says. "People are tiring of that."

John DePriest, AICP, director of planning for Chelsea, Massachusetts, says the essence of his community's appeal is its "proximity to Boston"—a city in the midst of a $1 billion arts building boom—"at less than Boston prices."

Another asset these suburbs can claim is affordability. In a sense, that is what landed many suburbs on the Lucy-Phillips list: Housing no longer desirable to middle-class families was ideal for immigrants starting out, or for the urban poor in search of safe neighborhoods and good schools. These days, however, affordability is starting to attract a more upscale set of buyers. In investment terms, poor inner-ring suburbs are the equivalent of penny stocks, capable of paying off big if the community's momentum is heading in the right direction.

Chelsea (pop. 35,100) still has plenty of problems, as its 65-page 2006 State of the City report will testify. Yet the difference, says DePriest, is palpable—and enriching for those who dared to move in when prices were at rock bottom. "When I started working here 11 years ago, the city was in receivership," he says. "You could have purchased a house here for one-tenth of what [houses] are going for now, though I grant that it would have needed a lot of work."

Now Chelsea even talks about requiring developers to build affordable units along with market rate ones. "Our city manager's goal is 1,200 new housing units, 15 percent affordable, in four years—and we're well on our way to that," DePriest says.

The picture is similar in National City, says Post: "The Southern California housing market is very strong, and we are more affordable than many places throughout the San Diego region," he adds.

Building amenities

If these suburbs had gorgeous waterfronts, they probably wouldn't be as poor as they are. Often they do have water, but it may not be very appealing. National City abuts the Pacific Ocean, but a military base occupies the shoreline. Chelsea is at the confluence of the Mystic River, Chelsea River, and Boston Harbor, but it's mostly a working waterfront.

Still, these communities are finding ways to exploit their location. National City has built 18- to 22-story residential towers with glorious views—once you're above the first few floors. East Palo Alto has attracted a high-end hotel that will offer water views—as well as jobs for local residents.

In Chester, Harrah's casino and racetrack will claim a stretch of what is now grim industrial riverfront. Chief planner William Payne dreams of extending that new energy further down the river.

"The waterfront is a real urban amenity," he says. "We recognized that 10 years ago and began thinking about how to capitalize on it. With Harrah's going in, we're hoping for some spin-off activity, and a lot of speculators are driving by, asking questions. We plan to develop some type of waterfront vision plan.

Not all of the suburbs on the list of 155 have waterfronts. But many of them have a certain special character in the form of old, if not historic, buildings. Of course, in many cases the age of the housing stock is the problem, not the solution. But Lucy suspects that some of these older communities probably have very interesting housing stock.

"I was in Buffalo recently, scanning real estate ads in the *Evening News*, and I could have bought three three-bedroom houses in Buffalo—three of

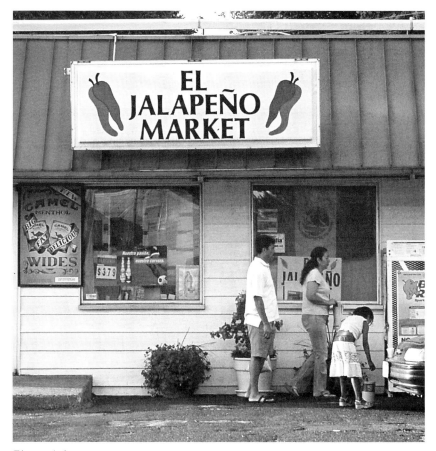

Figure 4-6
A favorable location and ethnic diversity help bolster Richfield, Minnesota.
Source: David Peterson

them—for $75,000," he says. "And worker housing built in the '20s can be quite nice."

That's certainly true in Chester, Irving says. "A 100-year-old power plant has been renovated into 400,000 square feet of first-class office space," she notes. "It's gorgeous. It was a brownfield, basically, and we made it into something usable and beautiful."

Diversity counts

Some officials in suburbs with low-income immigrants—and that includes a lot of them on the list, such as Langley Park, Maryland, where many residents are from El Salvador—are pitching diversity as a plus. These boosters think that younger people, in particular, may be attracted by the variety of cultures their communities can offer.

Hamtramck, Michigan, has become attractive to "artists and college-educated people who grew up in the 'burbs and wanted a different kind of life," says Mayor Majewski. "Now it's selling itself as a global city."

"All you have to do is walk a block from home—in my case, less than a block—to find a main drag full of small businesses," she says. "One place sells bread, another Bulgarian feta cheese; you pass kids from Bangladesh playing cricket, while others drive down the street playing Bosnian music. The streets are full of people on foot. And I think to myself, 'God, I love living here!'"

Flaunt it

Richfield, meanwhile, has awakened to the fact that it can leverage the success that lies beyond its borders. After all, it is right across the freeway from the Minneapolis-St. Paul International Airport and the Mall of America.

"We are looking at that Interstate 494 corridor and saying, 'That's fairly unique,'" says Bruce Palmborg. "When you factor in the airport and the mall, it's like, 'Wow! Richfield! Come on! Look what you've got going for you, guy!'"

Why not think in terms of the glamour of air travel, and offer, say, a jet-themed restaurant with views of arriving and departing planes? "We could turn and face into them," rather than ignore them, he says.

The revival of downtown Minneapolis is another opportunity, Palmborg says, especially because—as is often true of inner-ring suburbs—it means Richfield can tap into a new generation of light rail and bus rapid transit. Three new lines are either newly arrived or being planned for corridors in the Twin Cities' vicinity. Like Chelsea, Richfield is talking to job-rich neighbors about intersuburban circulators, which could help deliver modest-income workers to higher end employers.

"Richfield needs to play off those locational advantages," Palmborg says. "The challenge is to come up with creative thinking as we look out into the future. And that can be really difficult. We're so bound by the environment we're used to. How do we get up there?"

Many of the cities on the list of 155—a list Richfield doesn't make, but whose school district statistics make it a candidate for, if current trends continue—are facing the very same challenges.

"Do we have any planners who are 60 percent crazy and 40 percent stable?" Palmborg asks. "Let's get some vision going here. How do we play off these incredible assets at our doorstep?"

Cities like Richfield, he says, can't rest. "If you rest, you lose ground faster than you can regain it."

David Peterson is a reporter with the Minneapolis *Star Tribune*. This article was published in October 2006.

Resources

Background. A list of the 155 metro-area communities worse off than Detroit, together with other resources, can be found in *Tomorrow's Cities, Tomorrow's Suburbs*, $55.95 ($45.95 for APA members).

On the Web. "One-Fifth of the Nation: America's First Suburbs," by Robert Puentes and David Warren (Brookings, February 2006), is at www.brookings.edu/metro/pubs/20060215_First-Suburbs.htm.

A University of Minnesota site tracks racial change via 250 maps of 15 large metro areas. Choose "Minority Suburbanization and Racial Change," at www.irpumn.org/website/projects.

Background on major redevelopment projects in Richfield, Minnesota, is at www.ci.ricjfield.mn.us.

Images. The Hamtramck Star, with its often haunting images of one troubled community, is at http://hamtramckstar.com.

OldChesterPa.com is a site devoted to images and memories of a once-thriving inner ring suburb of Philadelphia: www.old-chesterpa.com.

City websites. A tour of the municipal websites of cities on the list of "155 worse off than Detroit" shows how dynamic, or forlorn, a city can look when glimpsed on the Internet, even though all of them are in much the same position. One site to learn from: National City, California (www.ci.national-city.ca.us), includes links from its home page to promising projects such as this one: www.centrocondos.com. Less professional, but with a video welcome from the mayor, is the site offered by Riverdale, Illinois: www.villageofriverdale.org.

NATIVE INTELLIGENCE
How urban Indians are faring.
By David Peterson

All morning Iwannah Bonnaha played the role of discreet intermediary, watching in silence as the Native American teenagers answered questions about their lives. But when it came to Ryan England, she couldn't stop herself.

"Did I hear you say you have a kid?"

"On the way," he said.

"And you're 16 years old?"

He nodded.

"Now, how'd that happen?" she asked, dryly.

Ryan reported that he had left home and was living with the family of the mother of his child—an arrangement whose air of adult complicity didn't impress Bonnaha, a Cherokee whose specialty is Indian education. Bonnaha works with hundreds of native students in two high schools in Tulsa, Oklahoma.

Will Rogers High School, located in a part of the city one resident referred to as "the 'hood," is a battered looking place. Although things have improved lately, Bonnaha says, as recently as last year she dreaded going to the school.

"The whole atmosphere was pressing in on me. There were no drinking fountains. The bathrooms were closed for part of the day, out of fear for what went on inside them. It was depressing. I didn't feel safe."

Yet, from what she hears, Bonnaha says, for Native Americans, "Oklahoma is utopia compared to a lot of states."

A study in contrasts

After the 2000 census data emerged, the Tulsa World searched through a huge array of numbers to find an American city that matched Tulsa most closely. The answer was Minneapolis. Even though the two metro areas differ in obvious ways, the cities themselves are close in size and share many characteristics. Both rank among the nation's top 10 in terms of Native concentrations.

Outside of Alaska, Tulsa has the largest percentage of Native Americans of any major U.S. city: eight percent. Minneapolis—ranking sixth, at just over three percent—is the most notable northern center for urban Indians, not least because it is the cradle of the American Indian Movement.

There are differences. Minneapolis is a liberal citadel. For years, the *Star Tribune*, Minnesota's leading newspaper, refused to use the nicknames

Figure 4-7
Members of the drum and dance group at Oh-Day-aki School in Minneapolis,
a charter school for at-risk urban Indians, perform at the Minneapolis Convention
Center during an American Diabetes Association "Diabetes Expo."
Source: David Peterson

"Redskins" or "Indians" when referring to the professional athletic teams in Washington, D.C., and Cleveland. In the fall of 2004 the leading vote getter for the Minneapolis school board was a 24-year-old member of the White Earth Band of Ojibwe with a degree in native studies. In 2005 a Seneca Indian bested all other candidates for the local library board by thousands of votes.

In contrast, Tulsa is a Bible Belt city with a pronounced cowboy identity: The sports teams at Oklahoma's two major public universities are the Sooners and the Cowboys.

Tulsa is decades behind Minneapolis in raising money for an Indian cultural center. And at Tulsa's Webster High School, football players race into battle as the Webster Warriors, making the school's principal, a Choctaw, ill at ease.

Yet the Native community in Tulsa seems to be doing better than its Minnesota equivalent. Indians in Tulsa earn incomes far closer to their neighbors' than do their counterparts in Minneapolis. In 2000, Native American median household income in Tulsa was about $30,000, or 86 percent of the city's overall median, according to the census. In Minneapolis it was $23,800, or 63 percent.

Indian kids in Minneapolis tend to turn in the worst academic results of any racial or ethnic group. But in Tulsa they lag behind only Asians and whites. Jean Froman, coordinator of Indian Education for the Tulsa schools, reports that about 500 Native students across the state were honored in 2006 for maintaining grade point averages of at least 3.9 on a 4-point scale.

Matching health data are harder to come by, but a 2004 report by Seattle Indian Health Board's Urban Indian Health Institute comparing health indicators in 34 urban areas (not including Tulsa) found Minneapolis close to the bottom nationally in several categories: worst in prenatal care, worst in smoking during pregnancy, second worst in births to teen mothers, second worst in infant mortality, second worst in alcohol-related deaths.

"Health conditions for Minnesota Indians are pretty nasty," says Kathy Davis Graves, author of a new edition of *Indians in Minnesota*, the latest installment in a typically Minnesota project: a monumental, decades-long effort by the state's League of Women Voters and others, including the University of Minnesota Press, to gather, and present to the outside world, the realities of Native lives. "It was a hard book to write: The conditions of Indian life are so depressing in many respects."

It's relative

That blue-state Minneapolis compares poorly with red-state Tulsa surprises few Native Americans in either place. Many in both cities have close, even family, connections in the other.

Anyone who says either "Minnesota" or "Oklahoma" is speaking an Indian language. Minnesota means "land of sky-blue waters"; Oklahoma means "land of the red man." The Oklahoma state license plate says "Native America." Signs along the edge of a freeway read, "Now entering Cherokee Nation." Oklahoma Indians hand you a map of the entire state, showing not a small handful of isolated reservations but Indian nations: Chickasaw, Choctaw, Creek, Cherokee, and Seminole, among many others.

Lillian Williams, an Indian educator in the Tulsa schools, and a mixture of Pawnee, Chickasaw, and Cherokee, says she was once addressing an assembly-sized group of schoolchildren. She began to name tribes, beginning with the smaller ones like the Kiowa, and asked students to stand as their tribal affiliation was called. Eventually about 60 people were standing, students and staff alike, in a group of around 400. Then she asked the Cherokees to stand. "Virtually everyone in the room stood up," she says, smiling at the memory. "The original 60 were just amazed!"

That doesn't mean they were correct. Some Native people in Tulsa speak wryly of the "Winabe tribe," a sly twist on the word "Wannabe" and a phenomenon well known to demographers, who are learning to mistrust increasingly fashionable claims of Indian ancestry. But intermarriage following forced moves to Oklahoma in the 19th century has made "Indianness" much hazier in Oklahoma than in Minnesota. One hears the term "identifiable Indian" far more often in Tulsa than in Minneapolis.

"Everyone in this state," says Iwannah Bonnaha, "is either Indian, or related to someone who is." Not true in Minnesota, where the atmosphere for Native people seems far chillier.

Isolated

Urban Indians are more segregated in Minneapolis than in Tulsa. In one census tract just south of downtown, 43 percent of all residents is American Indian, a level of concentration nearly three times as high as in any tract in Tulsa (15 percent).

Theron Warlick, a Tulsa city planner and a Cherokee, lived in Minneapolis for a year and a half while attending the University of Minnesota. A school for at-risk urban Indians was located just off campus. He found a more corrosive atmosphere in his adopted city than he ever encountered in his hometown.

Figure 4-8
A Native American family at a booth sponsored by the Indian Health Board of Minneapolis.
Source: David Peterson

"I was not there long before an acquaintance told me, 'The Indians are the ---- of Minneapolis,' he says, using a crude word for African American. "I was flabbergasted. We're not used to being treated as a minority. "

Indians feel isolated in the Twin Cities, says Valerie Larsen, the Urban American Indian Health Coordinator for the state Office of Minority and Multicultural Health. Still, she says, tens of thousands are drawn to the cities to find work.

Larsen, a member of the Pillager Band of Leech Lake Ojibwe (Chippewa), speaks from personal experience. "People ask me why I don't 'come home.' But the fact is I don't want to make rabbit snares. I want to shop at the supermarket. I want to live where there are real jobs."

A matter of money

Native Americans are a much smaller group in Minnesota, and if they live in the Twin Cities, they tend to be hundreds of miles from their home reservations in the northern part of the state. In Minnesota, with a Native American population of just over 80,000, almost half live in the Twin Cities metro area—nearly 13,000 in Minneapolis alone. About 19,000 live on reservations, mostly in the north.

*Figure 4-9
The Ancient Traders Market is one of the success stories of the American Indian Business Development Center. Source: David Peterson*

Oklahoma—with a Native American population of nearly 400,000—has no Indian reservations. Within the city limits of Tulsa, people talk about Cherokee territory and Osage territory in the same way that people in Minneapolis speak of Northeast or Uptown.

When Native American tribes began earning casino profits, the differences between the two states became starker. The big Oklahoma tribes are located near major cities and casino profits get spread around. Minnesota's biggest tribes are located far from population centers; casino profits tend to concentrate in the hands of the relatively small Indian groups living near the cities.

In a 14-page glossy publication called "Where the Casino Money Goes," the Cherokee people can learn how much casinos make and what becomes of the money. The emphasis is on employing Indians within the casinos, creating other jobs, and financing services such as health care and emergency assistance for the hungry or homeless. Cherokees are also dishing out $2 million per year for public education, a figure that tribal leaders say will rise "dramatically" with time.

That's not to say that casino profits have eluded Minnesota's Native Americans. Even on the Red Lake reservation, one of the poorest and most remote reservations in Minnesota—covering parts of nine counties in the northern part of the state—median household income during the 1990s rose 43 percent, inflation-adjusted, although the labor force swelled by hundreds of people returning in hopes of finding work.

Better times?

Among urban Indians there is some reason for optimism in Minnesota as well as in Oklahoma. One of the most important is in education. Graves, the author of the treatise on Minnesota's Indians, describes as "astonishing" the results educators are getting simply by pushing full-day kindergarten for children.

Between the fall of 2004 and the spring of 2005, full-day kindergarten made only a modest difference for white children, resulting in a total average academic achievement score of 299, versus 283 for half-day students. But for Indian kids the difference was immense: 244 versus 190.

The push for accountability in education, with greater emphasis on the basics, is also yielding results. Minneapolis school officials report that between 2001 and 2005, the rate at which Native American students scored at or above "proficiency" in reading in the third grade—a crucial moment, many educators say—rose from 34 percent to 46 percent. (The gap with whites closed modestly, from less than half to just over half.) Indians in the state as a whole did better: from 46 percent to 64 percent.

During the same period, indicators of health, bad as they are, were either stabilizing or improving in Minneapolis, according to the national survey conducted in Seattle.

Because Minneapolis's Indian community is so concentrated, improvements can be targeted to specific neighborhoods. Minneapolis and Hennepin County have spent millions upgrading Franklin Avenue, the heart of the native community. In 1999, Minneapolis chose Franklin Avenue as one of four commercial corridors to target for investment. Kristin Guild, AICP, principal project coordinator for the city, calls the result "the Franklin Avenue renaissance."

According to a case study she prepared, things began to turn around after the nonprofit American Indian Neighborhood Development Corporation took ownership of some property in the area. To replace a gas station that had ranked among the city's top five locations for volume of 911 calls, the corporation recruited a commercial bakery that now employs more than 80 people, many from the area. Aggressive management turned a strip mall from "a place of open drug dealing" to one that "draws people from around the city for breakfast and pottery."

A matter of pride

Most important, there is a spirit of cultural revival in both cities. Minneapolis now offers Anishinabe Academy, a public magnet school focusing on Native American culture and language that is also open to non-Native students. Indian educators in Tulsa speak proudly of the Indian language immersion schools that are emerging there, now that students are graduating from colleges with language degrees.

Gregory Pyle, chief of the Choctaw Nation, reported in a speech late last summer that Choctaw is now taught in 36 public schools, five colleges, and nearly 40 community classes. "Choctaw is not a dying language," he says. "It is a growing language."

In both cities a generation of college-educated Indians that emerged from the civil rights era is serving as mentors. "You can't save everyone," Iwannah Bonnaha says, but on the day she encountered young Ryan England, she had come to Rogers High to drop off flyers for Native kids about an upcoming field trip to a college in Kansas designed for them, and tuition free. She was serving as surrogate for the sort of college visits that middle-class parents handle for their own kids.

Indian kids in Tulsa—both middle class, like John Mark Griffith, whose father owns a pair of funeral homes, and not so middle class—say they are proud of their heritage. Ryan England says, "My brother has 'Native Pride' tattooed onto his arms. 'Native' on one arm," tracing a finger along his forearm, "and 'Pride' on the other." That identity truly pays these days, he says. "I'd rather be Indian than anything else."

David Peterson is a reporter with the *Star Tribune* in Minneapolis. This article was published in January 2007.

Who's Who

With the 2000 census, the federal government offered all Americans the chance to record their racial and ethnic pasts. Suddenly people didn't have just a handful of deceptively clear categories. They had hundreds of possible combinations.

But that also meant that anyone fancying himself as part Cherokee entered the data stream.

"It's very hard at this point to tell who exactly is an 'urban Indian,'" says Michael Woestehoff, a Navajo who serves as spokesman for the National Council of Urban Indian Health, an advocacy group in Washington, D.C. "Coming up on 2010, we have talked to the Census Bureau about finding out who actually is checking these boxes. We'd like to see to it that if you check that box, you must be a part of a federally registered tribe."

Native people in both Minnesota and Oklahoma speak of themselves as "card-carrying" or "enrolled" tribal members, unlike those who merely claim the affiliation, sometimes in hopes of receiving benefits.

The authors of a 2004 national report produced by the Seattle Indian Health Board, "The Health Status of Urban American Indians and Alaska Natives," stressed that "improvements in data collection pertaining to [native] race are urgently needed to better understand the true health status of Indians living both in urban areas and nationwide and to accomplish national goals of eliminating health disparities by the year 2010."

With those disclaimers, though, the Seattle report found that nearly 70 percent of the four million Americans recording themselves as Indians or Alaska Natives in the 2000 census lived in cities.

That analysis—of 34 urban areas served by Urban Indian Health Organizations, funded in part by the federal government's Indian Health Service—found that 25 percent were living in poverty, compared to 14 percent for all races combined. And, with some figures drawn from the 1990s, it reported that the rate of:

• Mothers younger than 18 was 80 percent higher than the rate for all races combined.

• Single mothers was 73 percent higher.

• Late or no prenatal care was 115 percent higher.

• Infant mortality was 33 percent higher, with sudden infant death syndrome 157 percent higher.

• Accidental death rates were 38 percent higher.

• Alcohol-related deaths were 178 percent higher.

• Diabetes was 54 percent higher.

Minneapolis, a leading center of Native activism, reported some of the worst statistics. Woestehoff cautioned against putting too much faith in such comparisons, however. A number of factors go into them, he says, including the care with which Indian ancestry is coded in different cities, the criteria used to define a person as Indian, and local funding, which affects the number of people treated.

SOVEREIGN NATIONS

Native Americans on the ladder to prosperity.

By Elizabeth Lunday

Thirty years ago, the Citizen Potawatomi Nation owned a few acres of land, a beat-up trailer, and $550.

The flimsy trailer was a miserable place in the heat of the Oklahoma summer, says John "Rocky" Barrett. His first decision when he was appointed to the tribal council in 1974 was to spend $200 on a window air conditioner. "I was the wastrel that spent all of the tribe's money," he jokes.

"Everyone asks, why didn't you save that structure?" says Barrett, who today leads the tribe as its chairman. "I couldn't wait to get rid of it."

The tribe's main office is not in a trailer anymore. Today, its headquarters are housed in a 65,000-square-foot facility up the road from the cultural center, health clinic, and golf course and across the street from the grocery store and casino. A second casino and resort recently opened a few miles away. The tribe has $350 million in assets, owns 5,000 acres of land, employs 2,200 people, and has a total impact on the local economy of more than $117 million, including salaries, tribal spending, and taxes collected by the tribe and remitted to local governments.

The Citizen Potawatomi story is an amazing tale of economic progress, but it's not a unique one. In recent decades, Native Americans across the U.S. have developed effective tribal governments, created profitable enterprises, and greatly improved their economic conditions.

Many Americans believe these economic strides are entirely the result of gaming, but casinos are only part of the story. "It's true that among gaming tribes per capita income grew at three times the rate of the U.S. economy as a whole" from 1990 to 2000, says Joseph Kalt, codirector of the Harvard Project on American Indian Economic Development. "What is surprising is that incomes in nongaming tribes also grew at about three times the rate of the U.S. economy."

That's not to say that Native Americans are all getting rich. Except for members of a few small gaming tribes, Indians lag behind the U.S. average on almost every socioeconomic measure, including median household income, child poverty, unemployment, and infant mortality. "You have to remember how far the tribes have to go," says Kalt. "If the growth of the 1990s continued, it would still take 50 years for tribal incomes to catch up."

The real key to tribal economic success seems to be self-governance, a term that applies both to federal law and to a philosophy of self-determination. "The policies of self-governance are the first that have worked in more than 100 years to provide sustainable economic development," says Kalt.

The experience of the Citizen Potawatomi demonstrates that tribes can use their sovereign powers to establish a government infrastructure, create enterprises that promote economic activity, and raise the living standards of tribal members as a whole.

From theory to reality

Native American tribes have always been sovereign—in theory. In the 18th and 19th centuries, the Potawatomi signed 44 treaties with successive French, British, and American governments, but the treaties provided little protection against land-hungry settlers. In 1838, the U.S. government forcibly relocated the group from Indiana to present-day Kansas. Other bands of the Potawatomi remained in the upper Midwest, moved to Canada, or settled elsewhere in Kansas.

Figure 4-10 Prosperity has allowed the Potawatomi tribe to move its headquarters from a cramped trailer to a modern office building. Source: Citizen Potawatomi Nation

In the 1860s, again under pressure from settlers, the Potawatomi sold their Kansas land and bought property in Oklahoma. They also adopted U.S. citizenship, becoming the Citizen Potawatomi, in an attempt to protect their property rights. It was a fruitless strategy—their land was given to other tribes or sold to white settlers. The tribe lost almost all the rest of its land in 1936, when the federal government dissolved all but one Oklahoma reservation.

So matters remained until the early 1970s, when a new self-determination policy was formulated by the federal government, partly in response to tribal assertions of sovereignty and partly out of recognition that previous policies had failed. The Indian Self-Determination and Education Assistance Act of 1975 allowed tribes to provide services and administer programs to their own members.

The law also fueled a new sense of responsibility. "Nobody else takes care of you as well as you take care of yourself," says Rhonda Butcher, Citizen Potawatomi director of self-governance.

Still, the road to self-governance was a rocky one. The tribe opened its first high-stakes bingo hall in the early 1980s, contracting with an outside management team to oversee the enterprise. Soon charges surfaced of mismanagement and faulty accounting. By 1984, the tribe had defaulted on its government contracts and the Bureau of Indian Affairs was threatening to suspend its constitution.

That's when Barrett's grandmother told him it was time for him to become tribal administrator. He says he didn't much want the job, but his family had a tradition of tribal leadership and his grandmother was the kind of matriarch who couldn't be defied.

Barrett immediately closed the bingo hall, blocking its doors with trucks and backhoes while the tribe went to court to declare the contract with the management company void and to gain control of the enterprise. The case wasn't completely settled until 1998, when the management company was ordered to pay the tribe $3.5 million in withheld funds. Barrett fired all but one tribal employee and set about creating a tribal government capable of leading his people into the future.

Reform

For decades, the Citizen Potawatomi were governed under a system imposed by the Oklahoma Indian Welfare Act of 1936. The act called for a strong executive and weak legislative body—but no independent judicial arm. Many tribes have found this system unworkable, according to the Harvard Project. After the 1984 crisis, the Citizen Potawatomi began amending their constitution to strengthen their legislative branch and develop an independent court system.

The tribe recognized the value of a viable judiciary. Businesses won't invest in a place where legal decisions are made on the basis of political favor or family loyalty. Many tribes, including the Citizen Potawatomi, adopted or amended the Uniform Commercial Code to meet their needs. Others, like the Navajo Nation, developed independent tribal courts on their reservations in Arizona, New Mexico, and Utah.

Still other tribes allow disputes to be settled by outside adjudicators or third-party arbitrators. Adjudication is controversial because it requires the tribe to sign a limited waiver of sovereign immunity. The White Mountain Apache Tribe, located on the Fort Apache Reservation in east central Arizona, c onsiders waivers a reasonable risk in exchange for outside investment, says Milfred Cosen, executive director of enterprise divisions for the tribe. "Some tribes are terrified to put any sovereignty at risk, but you've got to be willing to give up something to get something," he says.

The Citizen Potawatomi also developed an effective government structure, initiating an accounting system and an information technology network. The tribe takes pride in its financial department, which has received the Government Finance Officers Association certificate for excellence in financial reporting 17 years running. This sort of reform is crucial because tribes have to back up sovereignty by governing effectively, says Kalt.

The Citizen Potawatomi has also sought to increase the ties between its Oklahoma headquarters and non-Oklahoma tribal members. Because of moves during the Dust Bowl of the 1930s, the BIA's relocation programs of the 1950s and 1960s, and recent migrations, 18,500 of the 27,000 tribal members live outside the state, mostly in California, Oregon, Washington, Kansas, and Texas. The nation believed it could not succeed without the support of all members, no matter where they lived, says Barrett.

Figure 4-11
The FireLake Wellness Center offers diabetic education, nutrition training, and exercise facilities to tribal members and spouses. Source: Citizen Potawatomi Nation

The tribe created eight regions and appointed directors from each to serve on the tribal council. They also developed a plan to create a community center in each region. The first opened last year in Rossville, Kansas, and a second is planned for Southern California. The tribe intends to provide financial services, health care, and even housing in and around these centers.

Opening the centers outside their historic reservation boundaries is an unusual step for a tribe. Nearly half of all nonreservation Native Americans live in urban areas, yet this population is almost completely ignored by the Bureau of Indian Affairs, Indian Health Service, and tribal programs—and has suffered as a result. The unemployment rate of urban Indians is 2.4 times higher than that of urban whites and the poverty rate 3.9 times higher.

Not just gaming

The Citizen Potawatomi started its economic development program where many tribes do, with gaming. The tribal casinos are not just an opportunity for quick revenues, says Kalt; they are an assertion of sovereignty.

And gaming continues to be an important revenue source for the tribe, which operates two casinos. The first one, the FireLake Casino, located across the street from the tribal headquarters in Shawnee, looks like many Oklahoma casinos—a long, low building filled with jangling slot machines. It's clean and not too smoky, but it's no Caesar's Palace.

The newly opened FireLake Grand Resort is on another scale altogether, rising beside Interstate 40 like a vision of Las Vegas. The casino's monumental entrance, two-story interior fountain, and five-star steakhouse set the FireLake Grand apart from most of its Oklahoma counterparts.

Nevertheless, the tribe considers gaming income "found money," says Barrett. The strategy behind the FireLake Grand is to create a facility that can withstand a shakeout in the market without endangering the tribe's resources. "Gaming is a huge opportunity for us, but the debt [for casino construction] needs to be paid off as quickly as possible and those returns need to be put into something long range," he adds.

In fact, the tribe's long-term, noncasino investments are conservative. Before making an investment decision, we ask, "What's getting scarce, what attracts capital, what is recession proof?" Barrett says.

One of the first nongaming investments was the First National Bank and Trust, which the tribe bought in 1979. It was a small operation. One night, Barrett recalls, the tribal police officer who dropped off the night's take from bingo and slot machines called him in a panic. The night depository, overburdened with more than 100 pounds of coins, had crashed through the wall of the building, a modified trailer. Today the seven-branch bank is headquartered in a two-story brick structure in Shawnee and has assets and accounts totaling $150 million.

Economic diversification is the trend for most tribes. Only a few derive significant income from gaming enterprises. Fifteen percent of tribal casinos account for 69 percent of all tribal gaming revenues, according to the National Indian Gaming Commission, and fewer than half of federally recognized tribes (224 of 562) engage in gaming. Increasingly, tribes operate a variety of enterprises, ranging from farming, mining, and logging to manufacturing, tourism, communications, and construction.

Retail development has also attracted some Citizen Potawatomi investment money, although retail is a more pressing need for tribes based on reservations than those in cities. Members of the Citizen Potawatomi living in Shawnee can shop at the local Wal-Mart, but for Indians on isolated reservations in Arizona or Montana, buying basic supplies often means taking a long drive to town, says Levi Esquerra, program director at the Center for American Indian Economic Development.

The Citizen Potawatomi operate two grocery stores, FireLake Discount Foods in Shawnee and the FireLake Express Grocery in Tecumseh. The stores play a community service role, in addition to being profit-making enterprises, Barrett says. In Tecumseh, the tribe shares sales tax revenues with the municipality to support city services.

Figure 4-12
John "Rocky" Barrett heads a procession of elected members of the tribal council. Barrett is carrying an eagle feather, a symbol of leadership.
Source: Citizen Potawatomi Nation

It's notable that the stores and other Citizen Potawatomi businesses do not guarantee jobs for tribal members. Enterprises used as tribal employment services usually fail because they can't compete with nontribal businesses, according to the Harvard Project.

Finally, the Citizen Potawatomi have turned their backs on "per caps," the per capita payouts of profits that some tribes make to their members. Barrett points out that a $1,000 per cap to the tribe's 27,000 members would cost $27 million and leave each member with after-tax income of "less than the price of a new set of tires." Further, the tribe would have nothing left to invest in new enterprises.

Making entrepreneurs
The Citizen Potawatomi have a long history of small business ownership. In the 18th and early 19th centuries, tribal members operated ferry crossings, inns, and trading posts in the upper Midwest.

In general, however, extreme poverty, lack of capital, and a culture of dependency have suppressed the entrepreneurial spirit among Native Americans, says Tom Hampson, executive director of the Oregon Native American Business and Entrepreneurial Network, based in Tigard, Oregon.

Native American entrepreneurs face more than the usual challenges. Acquiring capital is complicated by the scarcity of banks in Indian communities and the difficulty of acquiring collateral by drawing on assets held in trust by the federal government. A 2001 study by the Community Development Financial Institutions Fund of the Department of the Treasury found a $44 billion gap between the existing and potential levels of investment in Indian country.

Community development corporations seek to fill this gap by providing small loans to Native-owned businesses. The Citizen Potawatomi opened a CDC in 2003 to support Native American businesses throughout Oklahoma and Citizen Potawatomi businesses across the U.S. To date, the group has made more than $3.9 million in loans to 68 businesses, creating or retaining 195 jobs.

A special kind of planning

Short-term economic development goals of the Citizen Potawatomi include the creation of an industrial park outside of Shawnee and a shopping center near the tribe's grocery store and headquarters. As the tribe continues to buy property and put it into tribal trust, issues of planning and land use will become increasingly important.

Few tribes have systematically addressed land use, says Hampson. On the White Mountain Apache reservation, for example, a community center was recently proposed for a site that the tribe's enterprise division considered prime commercial land. Milfred Cosen, the director of the enterprise division, says the tribe "put the cart before the horse" when it embarked on commercial development before developing a disciplined approach to land use.

Planning is complicated on Native lands by the historic distribution and treatment of land. In Oklahoma, the land holdings of many tribes are patch-worked across counties. On reservations, individual trust lands must be treated differently than tribal trust lands.

Then there are cultural considerations. The Ohkay Owingeh Pueblo, formerly known as the San Juan Pueblo, located just north of Santa Fe, New Mexico, recently completed a master plan that recognizes a 700-year-old culture, according to Deborah Webster, director of the Native American program for Enterprise Community Partners, which assisted with the plan.

The first project completed is Tsigo Bugeh Village, a 40-unit mixed income development that marries the principles of new urbanism with traditional pueblo architecture. The result is a complex of two-story units surrounding plazas that are aligned with the equinox and solstice sunrises.

Native planners have the opportunity to combine contemporary planning practice with an appreciation of traditional culture, says Ted Jojola, the Regents' Professor of Community and Regional Planning at the University of New Mexico and chair of APA's Indigenous Planning Division. "Whatever we do today should be informed by the past and should help us understand how we're responsible for the present and the future," he says.

Under assault

As John Barrett sees it, economic progress can have a risky consequence: It makes Native Americans an economic threat. "The aboriginal people of this continent have never been allowed to profit at the expense of those who came later," says Barrett.

The result, says Barrett, is that sovereignty is under assault from all sides. Harvard Project researchers agree, citing recent Supreme Court decisions and congressional proposals that chip away at tribal powers. In a 2001 case, *Nevada v. Hicks*, the Court ruled that states may regulate the activities of tribal members on tribal land. In a 2005 ruling, the Court held that lands owned by the Oneida Nation in New York were subject to local property taxes. Disputes are ongoing as to whether tribes are subject to federal labor laws and environmental regulations.

"Congress has plenary power over tribes, which means that at the stroke of a pen we go away as a government," says Barrett. But the same force that exposes the tribe to danger can also be its salvation, he says. "Economic power and political power are one and the same," he adds. "That Indian tribes have received some degree of political justice is only because of economic power."

Barrett's mission is to continue to improve the economic status of his people, partly by increasing their political clout.

Elizabeth Lunday is a freelance writer based in Fort Worth, Texas. This article was published in November 2006.

Resources

Learn more. Citizen Potawatomi Nation: www.potawatomi. org. White Mountain Apache Tribe: www.wmat.nsn.us. Harvard Project on American Indian Economic Development: www.ksg. harvard.edu/hpaied. Center for American Indian Economic Development: www.cba.nau.edu/caied. Oregon Native American Business and Entrepreneurial Network: www.onaben.org. Enterprise Community Partners Native American Program: www. enterprisecommunity.org/majorinitiatives/nativeamerican/index.asp. APA Indigenous Planning Division: www.planning. org/indigenous.

5

Katrina Victims

Natural disasters strike all over the world, but Americans assume we're prepared for our own emergencies: Just send in the National Guard and the Red Cross to clean things up and comfort the afflicted.

Hurricanes Katrina and Rita shocked the nation out of its complacency in the summer of 2005. Levees broke and people died because they couldn't escape the resulting floodwater—many of them because they lacked transportation. More than one-quarter of the population of New Orleans (about 130,000 people) was carless when Katrina struck.

The people of New Orleans and the Gulf Coast are still feeling the effects of the storms. In 2007, New Orleans's population was only half what it was before the storms and floods. Many families have dispersed and may never return.

Whether they reside in New Orleans or elsewhere now, the children who lived through the hurricanes are coping with disruption: broken families, missing friends, bad memories, fear. Schools and social agencies are trying to recapture a sense of stability while the surrounding community makes hard choices about how to rebuild.

Figure 5-1
Carless and frustrated in New Orleans. Flood victims photographed on
August 31, 2005, under a New Orleans highway approach as they wait for
buses. Source: Win Henderson/FEMA photo

EVACUATION AND EQUITY

A post-Katrina New Orleans diary.

By John Renne

FRIDAY, AUGUST 26, 1:33 P.M. Parents were moving their college-age children into dormitories and apartments at the city's colleges and universities. On the Elysian Fields bus, I talked to the father of a University of New Orleans freshman from California. The son was the first in his Hispanic family to attend college. Neither the father nor I had any idea that within hours thousands of people without access to cars, including many parents, students, tourists, and elderly, disabled, and low-income residents, would be stranded below sea level as a category four hurricane pummeled the city.

Just days earlier, I had met my first class at UNO. I was the first professor of transportation planning hired in decades at the only accredited planning program in the state of Louisiana. I had been attracted to New Orleans because its mixed use neighborhoods gave my wife and me the possibility of a car-free, or at least car-minimizing, lifestyle. We found an apartment on St. Charles Avenue, where I could hop onto the historic streetcars and transfer to the bus to get to work.

After riding public transit for a few days, I quickly learned a few things about transportation in New Orleans:

• The St. Charles line is the oldest continually operated streetcar line in America—and it's slow because car traffic bisects the route at every block. Often, an unaware motorist would pull in front of the streetcar, causing an accident and major delay. Still, both locals and tourists regularly use the line because it serves an important corridor within the city.

• Timetables for transit service are merely suggestions. A trip that takes 15 minutes by car can take an hour on the transit system. I didn't mind because I could use the time to read, grade papers, or just relax.

• Most middle-income residents long ago abandoned the transit system unless they had a direct connection, enjoyed the journey (like me), or were headed downtown or to the French Quarter, where parking is scarce. The most likely riders are transit's captive market (low-income, elderly, or carless). The same groups would be the most effected by Katrina.

SATURDAY, AUGUST 27, 8:47 A.M. After an evening spent enjoying the food and culture of our new city, my wife and I woke up to a call from our landlord: "There's a big hurricane warning, but don't worry; it will probably miss us." Obviously, my landlord was wrong.

The evacuation actually went rather smoothly. Early hurricane threats had served as practice runs, creating traffic jams that stretched all the way to Baton Rouge. But they showed local governments the need for an effective contraflow system for evacuation.

And despite the media reports to the contrary, the system worked during Katrina. People like me who had access to cars were able to evacuate in time. It took me five hours to reach the state capital, not bad even for a journey that normally takes about an hour. The third of the city's population that did not have access to cars was out of luck. Elderly, disabled, and low-income residents, as well as tourists without cars, had no evacuation options.

During the evacuation, the local radio stations gave advice on using the contraflow system. I heard nothing, however, about evacuation for residents without cars. I called the station and asked on air what the plan was for those people. A few moments later, I heard Mayor Ray Nagin telling people to go to the Superdome.

Two months later, on a flight from New Orleans to New York, the woman sitting next to me said she had heard me on the radio. She was angry that local officials had failed to evacuate the carless and proceeded to describe how she and her teenage son had waded through three feet of rising water in the middle of the night to escape their flooded home in the Upper Ninth Ward.

Sunday, August 28, 11:17 a.m. I finally got through to a television news station in New Orleans to ask why the city was not evacuating carless residents by buses or Amtrak. The voice at the other end responded, "Man, the last train left yesterday and we're packing up and running for our lives."

No surprise

The problems should not have come as a surprise.

The 2004 New Orleans Transportation Master Plan acknowledges that low income and lack of transportation could hinder the evacuation of many local residents. When Hurricane Georges threatened in 1998, only 27 percent of Orleans Parish residents evacuated; in neighboring Jefferson Parish, 45 percent of the residents got out. The plan notes that only 16 percent of Orleans Parish residents with an income below $25,000 evacuated, as compared to 54 percent of those with an income of over $80,000.

The plan recommends that the city and the Regional Transit Authority work together to facilitate the evacuation of those with limited mobility. The document calls on local churches, businesses, and nonprofit groups to provide transportation to those without cars or with special needs.

According to the plan, several entities—the Red Cross, the U.S. Department of Homeland Security, the New Orleans Public Health Department, the city's Office of Emergency Preparedness, and a nonprofit group called Unity for the Homeless—were in the process of creating a strategy to use Amtrak and city buses to evacuate 25,000 to 30,000 people in the event of a hurricane.

That part of the plan was never implemented because the city did not have regional agreements in place with the receiving sites. Adding insult to injury, 197 of the RTA's transit buses and 24 of its 36 lift vans were destroyed in the Katrina flood.

Figure 5-2 A flooded downtown street shot on August 30, 2005. Source: Marty Bahamonde/FEMA

Months before Katrina struck, the Operation Brother's Keeper initiative was launched. This initiative, which makes use of faith-based networks, was intended to team up carless residents with car owners in emergencies. Sad to say, this initiative was also not yet fully operational when Katrina hit. Only one church had implemented the plan.

Evidence shows that those who died in the flood were the most defenseless. In particular, the inadequate preparation for evacuating carless residents cost the lives of many seniors who were living independently but could not climb to safety or swim to save themselves.

A national problem

Officials at all levels of government failed to adequately plan for and respond to one of our nation's greatest challenges. Although Louisiana officials took the heat in Washington, D.C., for their failure to plan for evacuation, research is showing that the New Orleans plan was actually better than the evacuation plans of most major American cities.

Last September, I began a project to collect data on the nation's 50 largest cities to evaluate how their evacuation plans addressed the carless. I could find no evacuation plans for 26 cities. For those cities with plans, information concerning the carless ranged from nonexistent to a detailed description of pickup locations. For most cities, finding the information was a challenge. There is little uniformity in the various plans' provisions for evacuating the carless.

Only five cities included detailed provisions for carless residents in their plans. New York, Boston, Washington, Miami, and Honolulu said they provided specific pickup locations. Some cities, such as Jacksonville, have a special medical needs registration for evacuation. People on the list are called during an emergency.

A common misconception is that the risk was higher in New Orleans because of its large share of carless residents (130,000 residents, 27 percent of the population). In fact, seven cities, including Washington, D.C. (37 percent), Baltimore (36 percent), Philadelphia (36 percent), Boston (35 percent), Chicago (29 percent), and San Francisco (29 percent) have a higher percentage of carless households. In New York City, 56 percent of the population, or about 4.3 million residents, was carless in 2000. Across the nation's 50 largest cities, over 10 million residents are carless.

What we need to do

Evacuation planning in America needs to consider the carless, particularly the elderly and disabled. This need is increasingly important in a post-September 11 world. Moreover, the aging of our population means that more people will be at risk in the future compared to today.

Cities across the U.S. can learn from the success of the contraflow plan, which allowed traffic to use both sides of Interstates 55, 59, and 10 to flee New Orleans. It took cooperation between local and state governments, as well as cooperation between transportation officials in both Louisiana and Mississippi. America can also learn from Katrina by asking how the carless in their own regions would cope with a massive evacuation. Planners at every level of government need to start a dialog about how to create an efficient and resilient transportation system.

This dialog must include experts in other fields—including health care, housing, and social services. As many observers have noted, Katrina was as much a human disaster as a natural disaster. It will take a great deal of planning to ensure that all cities in America are prepared for the next big crisis.

John Renne is an assistant professor of urban and public affairs and director of the transportation center at the University of New Orleans. This article is based on a speech he gave at the annual meeting of the Transportation Research Board, sponsored by the TRB Environmental Justice in Transportation Committee. This article was published in May 2006.

THE KATRINA KIDS

Children are still suffering the aftermath of the 2005 hurricanes.

By Coleman Warner

They pulled out before dawn that Sunday, westbound, little more than a half-day ahead of Hurricane Katrina's approaching black-and-gray cloud bank.

Like so many others from New Orleans, the Schully family—with four children, ages 11 to 16—packed for just a few days, expecting to return quickly to a smattering of downed tree limbs and utility lines. They had no idea that a canal floodwall would crumble barely a mile from their home in the Lakeview neighborhood, sending a torrent of water four feet deep through their living room, or that even deeper waters would engulf much of their city, bringing ruin to countless things they cherished.

Four young people who had known an idyllic existence just a short walk from Lake Pontchartrain were unprepared for a storm surge that would shove water through neighborhoods rich with old architecture and parks and deeply rooted families. In the days following the flood, the Schully children sat in a Houston hotel room, stunned at television images of a flooded and paralyzed city, worrying about the family cat, Domino, which they had been unable to catch before the hurried evacuation.

"I freaked out," says Catherine, now 16. "I was terrified about Domino."

The Houston stay began a one-year odyssey for the family of Barry Schully, a mechanical engineer, and his wife Ellen, a former teacher, one that would include brief stays in Baton Rouge and Mandeville, on Lake Pontchartrain's north shore. The year brought anxiety and social adventure for the Schully children, and it would be followed by a painstaking transition when the family returned home in September 2006, before repair work on their home was complete.

The Episcopal school the children had attended in their neighborhood, St. Paul's, had been wrecked by floodwaters. Moldering homes, many of them not yet gutted, filled the landscape. City services were threadbare at best, with police relying on National Guard support. Domino, having been rescued by a neighbor after flood waters receded, was killed by another animal, most likely a raccoon. The Schully children, relieved to see old friends and schoolmates, would nevertheless spend many months in temporary or badly damaged school facilities.

The Schully experience is like that of thousands of other families who are trying to reconnect with their city. More than two years after the storm, New Orleanians face a setting of battered streets and parks, frayed medical services, hit-and-miss restoration projects for public buildings, and recovery planning efforts that so far have produced few visible results.

For the Schully children and many others, the hurricane and its aftermath had a distinctly silver lining. They learned hard lessons about adapting to change, found out they could make friends in strange new settings. They feel closer to each other and to their parents, more appreciative of their city and its culture. Through community service projects, they have a chance to help bring a great American city back to life. But talk to parents and expert observers, and they will say children are also continuing victims of a halting recovery, still waiting for broad evidence that the city is healing, still troubled by flood-damaged neighborhoods and odd housing circumstances.

Kids' needs

Babs Johnson isn't impressed by official rhetoric about taking care of the post-disaster needs of children. A New Orleans native and longtime volunteer child advocate in court settings, Johnson is furious that the city and federal governments didn't move quickly to restore recreation centers, that medical services for poor children are now especially hard to secure, that for many months flooded public school buildings were left open to the elements, unsecured, the private records of children scattered and easily plucked up by anyone who happened by.

Johnson noted that the Allstate Foundation has agreed to put up $70,000 to repair a playground in her Uptown neighborhood that could have been restored through the New Orleans Recreation Department and federal grants—and adds that the delayed repair project fits a long-term pattern of neglect.

"The government is a joke," she says. "It's almost to the point where you just have to close your eyes and do what you have to do."

Issues directly impacting the quality of life of children, such as getting more child care centers back in operation, seem overshadowed by "adult problems" such as securing Road Home grants for rebuilding homes, Johnson says. "Instead of being at the forefront of every issue, [children are] at the back," the activist says.

Others stress that recovery issues transcend age lines, that by helping adults to rebuild a home, for example, you help bring stability to their children. Still, many argue that more concentrated attention should be paid to the needs of children, who often suffer in silence or act out through verbal outbursts or even criminal behavior.

Nonprofits and churches have stepped in to do what they can to help storm victims, and local officials are beginning to tap infrastructure repair grants from the Federal Emergency Management Agency. But more remains to be done before child-friendly conditions are to be found in the storm zone.

Refurbished classrooms are only a start, says Doris Voitier. As superintendent of public schools in St. Bernard Parish, a marsh-laced section downriver from New Orleans that saw nearly 100 percent of its buildings flooded out, Voitier earned national acclaim for her ferocious drive to repair and reopen a handful of schools in the months after the 2005 storm.

Figure 5-3
The Schully family enjoys a quiet moment at their house in the Lakefront neighborhood of New Orleans. At either end are parents Barry and Ellen (holding Rocki). Between them are daughters Catherine, Amy, and Lauren. Source: Lashlee Warner

The rebuilding effort, one initially launched with little help from the federal government, has produced beautiful facilities where, once inside, "it looks like nothing happened," she says. But a panorama of destruction can be found near restored schools, with FEMA trailers and shattered businesses still dotting the landscape. St. Bernard's sole hospital remains shuttered. And Voitier still sees evidence of emotional upheaval in a significant number of the thousands of children who have returned to St. Bernard schools.

Contrary to perceptions elsewhere in the U.S., things are far from back to normal for the children of Katrina, Voitier says. "I see many times anger, especially in older children, teenagers. I see frustration. We're seeing behaviors that we've never seen in our children before—outbursts, and sometimes sexual behaviors."

Voitier says she is thankful that extra counselors have been made available to public schools through a medical services arm of Louisiana State University. "I think a lot of it is a product of cramped living conditions, listening to their parents' frustrations and arguments. Without some additional help for children, we might see long-term effects."

Thousands of families displaced by Katrina are still gone and may never return, despite pleas from government figures, from Gov. Kathleen Blanco to New Orleans Mayor Ray Nagin, that they reclaim their old homes and neighborhoods and pitch in with the rebuilding mission. Children now resettled in Atlanta or Houston or Chattanooga or other far-flung communities—with virtually every state having taken in storm refugees—often see new opportunities for themselves in school or in new social circles even as they face difficult adjustments. For children who have managed to return, there was relief in simply being home again, but Katrina has changed nearly everything, and life in the Big Easy is anything but.

"We're seeing a lot of resilience, but at the same time we're seeing a lot of suffering and a lot of symptoms," says Howard Osofsky, chairman of the psychiatry department at LSU Health Sciences Center.

Bad memories

The post-Katrina strains on young people come in many forms, health experts and educators say. Some children still struggle with memories from a frantic evacuation or from being trapped for days in a city engulfed by water and misery. A substantial number lost relatives or saw bodies floating in city streets. Some cry at the noise of an ordinary rainstorm, flashing back to the hurricanes.

In countless instances, children grieve over the loss of a pet, family pictures, clothes—and a home that they once considered a safe haven. Extended family networks that provided daily support before the storm were torn, as grandparents or aunts and uncles moved away or to other parts of the New Orleans area.

There are fewer things for young people to do, as many parks and libraries and movie theaters were destroyed by floodwaters and have yet to be replaced. Health habits have deteriorated as stressed families watch more television and consume more fast food. Severed friendships and new school settings, even refurbished facilities, tend to bring new anxieties.

Fragmented or cramped housing poses a major problem, as New Orleans and surrounding communities face a shortage of quality affordable housing and many families—waiting for Road Home grants or insurance settlements, or simply unable to cover rising construction costs—haven't managed to rebuild their homes. At Cohen High School in New Orleans's Central City neighborhood, a freshly rebuilt public school with nearly 600 students, principal Arlene Kennedy says about half of her students face an ad hoc housing arrangement at home, often with no reliable adult present.

"In my use of a conditional suspension (for disciplinary problems), it's my opportunity to bring a parent in and say, 'Okay, let's play your part in whatever is going on with this child,'" says Kennedy, who was recruited from South Carolina by New Orleans's Recovery School District. "You'd be amazed (how many children say), 'I don't even have her number, I haven't seen her since last week.' or 'Me and my sister have an apartment together, can I bring my sister?'"

Such disjointed living arrangements, most prevalent among poor families, are cited by state Superintendent of Education Paul Pastorek as one of the lingering "indirect effects" of the hurricane, alongside greater difficulties in accessing services from medical and mental health professionals whose local ranks were thinned dramatically after the storm.

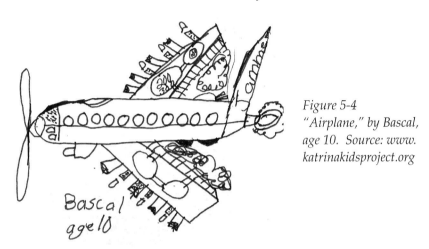

Figure 5-4
"Airplane," by Bascal,
age 10. Source: www.
katrinakidsproject.org

One veteran pediatrician, Daniel Bronfin of Ochsner Clinic, sees a greater incidence of depression and unease among young people he cares for, and notes a tight correlation between how a child and his or her parent, or caretaker, are faring. If the adults in a household are recovering and hopeful, chances are the children are too, and the reverse is also sadly true, he says.

Some numbers

In one of the few studies that provides a broad indicator of how adults rate their own recovery track, a fall 2006 survey of 1,504 adults in four area parishes by the Henry J. Kaiser Family Foundation found that 52 percent rated their financial situation as worse than before Katrina, while 37 percent reported disruption in their housing or social network, and 36 percent said their access to medical care had been compromised.

Among those interviewed, 23 percent reported a personal toll in temper, alcohol use, or marriage tension, while 19 percent said their physical health had deteriorated and 16 percent reported mental health troubles.

More than half of those surveyed cited problems in at least two of the storm-effects categories.

"Most of these impacts are not transitory, not problems that evaporated as the city dried," concluded an analysis of the survey, published in May 2007. "Instead, they are problems still being faced every day in New Orleans. And they are problems layered into a community that already faced considerable socioeconomic challenges before Katrina's winds neared the Gulf Coast."

Lingering impacts were felt most strongly in the African American community. Among black residents answering the survey, 59 percent said their lives were "very" or "somewhat" disrupted, in contrast to 29 percent of white residents.

Children's stories

Many parents take pride in their ability to hold their families together in the midst of a chaotic episode in American history. But they also worry that their own fight with recovery is affecting their children. Such is the case with Barry and Ellen Schully, who felt compelled to get back to New Orleans and rebuild their lives partly because Barry also served as a board member of the flooded out Episcopal school.

The couple says their eldest son Charles, now 18, was deeply troubled by a keen understanding of the stress his parents faced. He ultimately passed on the chance to attend college in California, opting instead to enroll at Louisiana State in nearby Baton Rouge. Catherine Schully recalls that "it was really hard seeing Mom cry so much." And Amy, now 13, wonders if she and her siblings made matters worse for their parents by pushing for a return: "We were just dying to come back," she says.

Fierce debate over the adequacy of counseling and other mental health initiatives, mostly paid for with federal dollars and delivered at the school level, is fueled by reports that more than 40 percent of children assessed in Orleans, St. Bernard, and Plaquemines parishes, the county-level jurisdictions hit hardest by flooding, meet criteria for mental health treatment. Beyond the school setting, mental health services are stretched thin.

A documentary titled Katrina's Children, produced by Babs Johnson and Laura Belsey, a New York-based filmmaker, reaches beyond statistics to provide intensely personal interviews with more than a dozen children affected by the storm, representing a mix of ethnic groups and family income levels. The film depicts devotion to place and hope for better days, but also offers disturbing glimpses into trauma.

In the film, Erica Jackson, a Central City resident who was 10 at the time of her interview, talks of taking refuge in a two-story house in her Central

Figure 5-5
Summerbridge New Orleans, a year-round program for school children,
reopened last summer after a hiatus following Hurricane Katrina. Source: Ellis
Lucia © 2007 The Times-Picayune Publishing Co.

City block when the storm hit, of later seeing bodies and animal carcasses in floodwaters. She begins to speak in rapid-fire fashion and then cries as she walks with the interviewer through her neighborhood, now left trash-strewn and mostly abandoned:

"I used to love to swim, but I don't swim any more," she says. "It took my house, it took everything, and it's just not fair. . . . My parents, they just don't know what's going on. They keep on asking me what's wrong and everything. They just try to make it go away. I try to see a counselor at school, but they can't make it go away. Nothing can make it go away."

Dakota Davis, 13 when he was interviewed, grieves over the loss of his home in the Plaquemines Parish community of Buras, a settlement virtually wiped from the map by a towering storm surge south of New Orleans. But Davis, whose family has relocated to Picayune, Mississippi, an hour's drive from gulf waters, is even more torn over the scattering of his playmates.

Speaking quietly in the documentary, he weeps also: "Sometimes, I just wonder why it happened, why my house got taken away. I know it's not my fault, but I could have changed things. I could have quit being mean. I could have been more grateful for what I've been given. And I could have not took my friends for granted. Everything was so nice and happy down there, and I was always playing with my friends. We were always excited, and we always got to play, and then this happened, and now I don't see any of them. It's just devastating to have everything you love taken from you. It's not always easy for me to wake up and go to school."

Rebuilding the schools

Facing the greatest displacement of students that America has seen since the Great Depression after Katrina, education officials pleaded with school systems elsewhere in Louisiana, and in other states, to take in the children. They also faced a daunting rebuilding task back in New Orleans. But now it seems that educators are finally reclaiming a measure of stability. School system officials report they are making progress in navigating a cumbersome FEMA process for securing millions of dollars for storm-related construction. Almost without exception, hard-hit universities are slogging through building repairs and gradually increasing enrollment figures.

After major delays in carrying out critical building repairs in the first year after Katrina, the Recovery School District in New Orleans, with hands-on prodding from state Superintendent of Education Pastorek and technical help from the Louisiana National Guard, has earned praise by getting a network of schools fixed up and back in use—with extra attention given to rundown restrooms and kitchen facilities.

Innovation has been ushered in, too, by the post-Katrina era. Charter schools that give parents more choice, and allow varied teaching methods, have flourished in New Orleans; essentially, they have created a closely watched education laboratory. Young, highly motivated teachers from across the country are responding to calls for help.

On parallel tracks

But if visible progress is being made on the educational front, citizens have seen little impact from broader planning endeavors. Efforts to craft a specific recovery agenda for New Orleans neighborhoods, beginning with Mayor Nagin's Bring New Orleans Back Commission soon after the storm and culminating with the Rockefeller Foundation-backed Unified New Orleans Plan in the fall of 2006, produced billions of dollars in suggested projects, many involving parkways and libraries and community centers that could enhance the daily lives of young people. But the effort, by most accounts, was largely detached from school site planning by the Recovery School District and Orleans School Board, which moved forward on a later timetable.

Further, while the Louisiana Recovery Authority has dedicated more than $100 million from federal block grants to help start implementation of the plan, New Orleans officials moved slowly in naming their priorities—and, more importantly, in unleashing architects and building crews.

A regional plan of the Louisiana Recovery Authority, pushing such ideas as commuting by rail and flood-savvy development codes, focuses more on how citizens might live smarter decades from now than on meeting their needs two years after hurricanes Katrina and Rita. "It may not be a 15-year-old that will benefit from it," says Donna Fraiche, chairwoman of the recovery authority's planning task force. "It may be a five-year-old that will benefit from it 10 years down the road."

Steven Bingler, a New Orleans planner and architect who coordinated work on the Unified New Orleans Plan, says the exercise reinforced calls for the creation of schools that can serve as around-the-clock community centers, acting as a surrogate parent for children with added medical, mental health, and mentoring programs. But Bingler, whose firm Concordia Architects also is providing long-range planning advice for Orleans public school officials, conceded it will be years before the community schools idea can take shape in his city. Futuristic exercises mean little, he says, to children who are still waiting for direction and improved public services.

"In the meantime, people are scrambling around, doing what they've always done—the best they possibly can," says Bingler, who finds signs of desperation in young New Orleanians who resort to burglary and gunplay. "I certainly don't think that planning is a solution for short-term needs."

What the kids suggest

Many students are quick to pitch their own ideas for how New Orleans should be rebuilt, and they often strike a remarkably hopeful tone, even in the midst of personal loss.

At Cohen High, senior William Branche is trying to overcome what he calls educational and social disruptions caused by temporary stays in Texas and Michigan after Katrina, then by his brief enrollment in another New Orleans high school that he says had low standards. Branche, 17, lost nearly all his possessions when his father's home in eastern New Orleans flooded to the ceiling. For a year, he lost contact with most of his friends. But he says Katrina "didn't destroy my life" and that he sees fresh prospects for positive change in New Orleans.

"A lot of the schools are being rebuilt better, and a lot of business is coming down here just because, one, property is cheaper," says Branche, a part-time chef who also wants to buy, fix up, and resell blighted houses. "A lot of communities are pulling together now, where before. . . individual households kind of stuck to themselves. Now you have the whole neighborhood going out, gutting a house, trying to make it look nice. You see more community effort."

Amy Schully, having returned with most of her classmates to a refurbished Episcopal school, says Katrina deepened her appreciation for family and fueled a budding interest in creative writing. "For me, the hurricane was a good thing," she says. "It changed me so much. I like to express my feelings through writing. I've been writing a lot lately. . . . I'm writing a book now."

At Katrina's second anniversary, the eighth-grader joined a few St. Paul's classmates at a somber public ceremony, held a few blocks from the point of the Lakeview floodwall break, now the site of a mammoth Corps of Engineers flood protection project. There, she recited a poem she had written about her Katrina journey, If Only, which reads in part,

> If only we all knew a storm was about to hit,
> If only we knew so much more was in store for us,
> If only we hadn't taken so many things for granted,
> How would we be now?

Watching from a short distance away on a grassy median, Amy's father was proud that his daughter could share her reflections. But he would later admit that he frets about Katrina's lasting impact on his teenagers.

"It forced them to grow up quickly, and they lost part of their childhood," he says. "You just don't know how it's going to affect them—mentally, psychologically, emotionally—as years go on . . . you just hope that it takes care of itself. They're always going to look back on it, tell their grandkids about it. The way my parents always talked about the Depression, I think they're going to talk about Katrina, and what they went through."

Coleman Warner is a staff writer for *The Times-Picayune*, covering Katrina recovery issues. Warner and his family recently moved back into their rebuilt Lakeview home. This article was published in January 2008.

Resources

Online. Find more on post-Katrina health issues at the Kaiser Family Foundation website: www.kff.org. A variety of information about Hurricanes Katrina and Rita is available at the Louisiana State University website: www.lsu.edu.

Index

Discussion Questions

1. Why are issues like homelessness, joblessness, immigration, and poverty considered to be planning issues?

2. How do past and current land-use policies and regulations contribute to some of the problems outlined in the book? Which traditional or nontraditional planning approaches could help?

3. How do global climate change and local planning intersect? Are there any special considerations for marginalized communities?

4. Of all the overlooked populations and problems identified in the book, which is the most challenging?

5. How do federal programs help address some of the issues noted in this book? How do they help or hinder local efforts?

6. Of the problems examined in this book, which are best left to private organizations to address rather than government agencies?

7. Choose a real or fictional city and describe a potential long-term planning strategy to address one of these issues. What short-term tactics might be successful?

8. Which marginal populations and issues are missing from *Overlooked America*? Are there any that don't belong?